WIN WIN

HELPING ORGANIZATIONS MITIGATE LEGAL RISK FOR THE COMMON GOOD

REBECCA SPOSITA, ESQ.

HiGHERLIFE
PUBLISHING & MARKETING

HigherLife Development Services, Inc.,

PO Box 623307, Oviedo, FL 32762

(407) 563-4806, higherlifepublishing.com

Edited by Esse Johnson

Published 2024

Printed in the United States of America

30 29 28 27 26 25 24 1 2 3 4 5

ISBN: 978-1-964081-21-2 (paperback)

ISBN: 978-1-964081-22-9 (eBook)

Library of Congress record: 1-14302286591

PRAISE FOR *WIN WIN*

Rebecca is one of the most loving, powerful, and high-integrity leaders I know. The fact that she uses her care and superpowers in service of protecting clients, standing for justice, and speaking the truth is a gift for our culture. Her writing is vulnerable, intelligent, and to the point as she invites the reader to see some of the most tricky situations through a new and more humane lens.

Anese Cavanaugh,
CEO Active Choices

This book is a must-read for claims folks and their defense teams, as well as human resource professionals. Rebecca explains the how and why her process can help mitigate (or eliminate) excessive and expensive litigation.

Paul Anderson,
Vice President Crum & Forster Insurance Company

This book is a well-structured and important handbook for boards and management groups of companies, with the author skillfully integrating her own story throughout. It provides valuable insights into the importance of human rights in the area of ESG, making it a must-read for a wide audience.

Katja Keitaanniemi,
CEO OP Corporate Bank Plc

Business leaders, HR practitioners and line managers can learn much from this book. Events in the workplace need to be seen from both the victim as well as the company perspective, and Rebecca successfully combines her personal account as well as legal expertise to seek win-win solutions that will help manifest a positive organizational culture in any workplace.

Ben Baxter,
COO Kenmare Resources

To the mighty Jane and John Does who have taught me the true meaning of courage. May your flames light a path toward a global culture of safety, equity, and accountability.

CONTENTS

Chapter 1   1
The Process Isn't Working

Chapter 2   9
I Thought I Was Prepared

Chapter 3   22
The First Step: A Trauma-Informed Response

Chapter 4   42
Unraveling the Facts

Chapter 5   90
Reforming the Process

Chapter 6   124
Safeguarding Your Organization's Reputation

Chapter 7   159
Seeing Complaints as Opportunities

Chapter 8   178
Consider an Apology

Conclusion   195
Appendix I   201
Appendix II   207
Appendix III   213
Acknowledgments   217

CHAPTER 1

THE PROCESS ISN'T WORKING

As a plaintiff's attorney and president of a large, well-known law firm in the United States, I've devoted my career to helping injured men and women seek justice through the American judicial system. Despite the common stigma that claimants are opportunists looking for money, those we see in our firm come to us after experiencing a legitimate personal injury, medical malpractice, or sexual assault. We only accept cases that we believe truly have merit and we are successful at winning the complainant compensation for their suffering.

Why, then, am I writing a book on how your institution can avoid a lawsuit and mitigate damages? Because I want organizations to respond to reports of wrongdoing in a more humane manner—and I'm going to show you why doing so is in your best interest.

The most recent comprehensive study calculating American litigation costs looked at 200 Fortune 500 companies and the findings were shocking.

"The <u>average</u> outside litigation cost per respondent was nearly $115 million in 2008, up 73 percent from $66 million in 2000. This represents an average increase of 9 percent each year," the report noted. The average legal fee alone for these companies was $60,577,443 with a median payout of $2,019,248 per case—significantly higher than comparable companies in other countries. What's more, discovery costs in America were on average one-quarter of legal fees. [i]

". . . when a potential plaintiff comes to our law firm seeking representation, their desire for justice almost always far outweighs their desire for money."

Litigation not only has a significant impact on a company's profits, but as our costs continue to climb, many find it more beneficial to simply leave the United States where prolonged litigation, exorbitant legal fees, and time- and cost-consuming discovery are unlike anywhere else in the world. We have nearly twice as many civil lawsuits as the U.K., three times that of Australia and Japan, and four times the rate of our neighbor, Canada. We also have more lawyers per capita than nearly any other country, with only one exceeding our rate. [ii]

---

[i] Lawyers for Civil Justice (2010), "Litigation Cost Survey of Major Companies," submitted by Lawyers for Civil Justice, Civil Justice Reform Group, U.S. Chamber for Legal Reform Group, Presented to Committee on Rules of Practice and Procedure, Judicial Conference of the United States, 2010 Conference on Civil Litigation, Duke Law School, May 10-11, 2010.

[ii] Ramseyer, J. Mark and Eric B. Rasmusen, (2010), "Comparative Litigation

Reasons for this high rate remain speculative, but as a litigation attorney I can tell you that when a potential plaintiff comes to our law firm seeking representation, their desire for justice almost always far outweighs their desire for money. They're not trying to shake you down. They're not chronic complainers and professional victims who will never be happy. They want to feel heard and be compensated fairly for their suffering.

Despite this, most executives, administrators, and in-house legal counsel respond to claims with an aggressive resistance. Rather than correct the problem, the goal is to control the narrative, save the organization's public image to safeguard the stock price, and minimize any settlement or judgment so future claims are discouraged. Their *modus operandi* is to answer to the complaint with suspicion. Searching for contributory negligence or other holes in the report, investigators seek any opportunity to deny responsibility and quickly defeat allegations. They exploit every possible weakness in the complainant's story and, of course, never apologize for fear of being perceived as admitting liability. For as long as possible they dismiss or ignore the complaint in hopes that it will go away.

Those institutional defenses often backfire. Rather than avoid, they wind up escalating costs, damaging reputations, and ensuring that the claimant pursues the claim as aggressively— and publicly—as possible.

BETRAYED BY THE SYSTEM:
A SECONDARY ASSAULT

When institutions fear that addressing the problem or admitting responsibility will guarantee a costly lawsuit, the tendency is to

---

Rates," Harvard, John M. Oliver Center for Law, Economics and Business, Discussion Paper No. 681, available online at: Microsoft Word - 11-07b- litigation.doc (harvard.edu).

do nothing and wait for the problem to disappear, or attempt to personally discredit the one coming forward. This is like a secondary assault to the person who has risked their safety and reputation by bringing the issue to light. The victim is already shaken and feeling unsafe. When they feel betrayed by the system they trusted to protect them, that betrayal causes another form of trauma. Trauma, as you'll see, powerfully impacts the reporting process itself. If someone feels betrayed by an entity they thought would have their back, primal instinct signals that our very survival has been threatened.[iii] The person who feels betrayed will likely seek justice elsewhere—in the courts, in the press or, in some tragic cases, through violence.

Instead of seeing the organization respond to the complaint constructively to protect its people and prevent future incidences, many who step forward become the target of institutional aggression. They may be branded liars, complainers, or opportunists, blamed for what happened, or just ignored. They find themselves battling a convoluted network of reporting procedures, telling and retelling their stories to new inquisitors at every stage, often brushed off like trivial annoyances, suffering humiliation as they're forced to continually relive the traumatic event and, worst of all, interrogated like criminal suspects. As the process unfolds they find that, rather than feeling heard and their concerns addressed, the process itself has re-traumatized them.

It's this further trauma, I've discovered, that often prevents early settlements, increases damage awards, and leaves a plaintiff feeling determined to proceed to trial—where jury awards can easily reach seven and eight figures.

I should know. I'm an experienced litigator and manage a firm with well over a hundred employees. In my administrative

---

[iii] Geher, Glenn and Nicole Wedberg (2020). *Positive Evolutionary Psychology: Darwin's Guide to Living a Richer Life*, Oxford University Press.

capacity I'm on the frontlines of handling internal and external complaints. My experience with clients has taught me a great deal about the pain and suffering they experience both from the incident itself and through the legal process. However, my deepest and perhaps most valuable insights have come through my own experience of reporting a personal assault. This experience taught me a dimension of personal injury reporting and litigation that I'd never fully appreciated. The reporting process re-traumatized me in a multitude of unexpected ways. What's more, I experienced this suffering through every stage of the process, something for which I was wholly unprepared despite my years of representing clients. If this re-traumatization could happen to me, a seasoned personal injury attorney, it can happen to anyone.

"The reporting process re-traumatized me in a multitude of unexpected ways."

It doesn't have to be this way. There is no reason someone making a report of wrongdoing needs to be treated inhumanely. Reforming the process from the first official report through litigation not only has the potential to help the plaintiff heal, but it can also reduce an institution's risks of litigation, potentially minimize damages, and protect the institution's reputation. Most importantly, by addressing complaints you're less likely to encounter them in the future.

THE COMMON RESPONSE IS NOT WORKING

Men and women throughout the nation come forward daily to report injuries they've suffered. Too often when people do come forward they discover the posters and fliers encouraging them to reach out for help, the assurances of protection, and the provision of a hotline were all hollow. The institutional process that follows is hardly straightforward and rarely, if ever, ends quickly. An already injured party finds themselves subjected to multiple interviews over months and sometimes years.

If you represent an organization and a claim comes your way, you should know that the more the complainant feels traumatized by the process itself, the more they can and will pursue further action. Therefore, I'm glad to share that I also learned something positive from my difficult experience. What began as a traumatic experience transformed into a constructive and insightful one. Eventually, I was able to work with the institution and provide my insight on a more effective and compassionate approach to handling complaints. By listening to how their process further traumatized me and made the situation more problematic for them, they were able to make important changes that better serve their community.

I hope to show that today's most common response to these matters is not working. When someone says they've been harmed, choosing to ignore, disbelieve, dismiss, or blame them won't make them go away. It will more likely provoke them to call someone like me, an attorney who will stop at nothing to ensure justice and probably a high financial recovery. They'll become more determined than ever to ensure that the matter does not go away quietly. In fact, they'll tell anyone and everyone who will listen.

So, what can you do to ensure that your company does not find its financial and human resources consumed by unnecessary litigation costs and adverse publicity? You may find my answer counterintuitive.

In the pages of this book, I'll show you a thoughtful approach that makes the claimant feel heard and their suffering acknowledged. Take heed to my advice, and you may well prevent a lawsuit because institutional responses at the earliest stages can shape the entire trajectory of the investigation. If you're quick to address internal systemic problems being brought to your attention, you can potentially ward off future lawsuits.

In this book we will examine how trauma shapes reporting and investigation, and how a trauma-informed response can transform the operation from an adversarial one heading to the courts to a partnership with the common goal of an effective and fair resolution. In the next chapter, I'll tell you my story so you can see firsthand how even a successful, strong-minded, and seasoned attorney can be wholly unprepared for the trauma caused by an unexpected assault.

CHAPTER 2
I THOUGHT I WAS PREPARED

We'd just had dinner at the Harvard Club, dining on kaleidoscopic salads, tiny plates of seared scallops, and larger plates of poached salmon set atop colorful swirls of vegetable purees. I had joined the world's academic elite and found myself in a place where women were not even permitted until 1973, the year before my birth. To this day few have the honor of entering the beautiful Georgian mansion carpeted in exquisite golden patterns where I now supposedly belonged, its mahogany walls sealing us from the outside world.

I'd worked hard to be among the women welcomed into the Harvard Club in the twenty-first century. When I first applied to colleges, Harvard wasn't even on the horizon. I grew up focusing more on friends and sports than school, so I spent time at a community college and a couple different universities before I developed a love for lifelong learning. It wasn't until after I'd married and had my first son that I decided to go to law school.

After passing the bar and becoming a successful litigator, my horizons began to change. Whether it was medical malpractice, disability claims, discrimination, sexual harassment, or assault, I learned how to use the law to give voice to some of our most marginalized citizens. Then came Larry Nassar, a professor and physician at Michigan State University, who had assaulted hundreds of young female athletes under his medical care. As their attorney, I helped some of these young women to navigate the bewildering and complex legal system, making them not nearly whole but financially compensated for the horrific abuse they'd suffered. These were women who had achieved extraordinary success in their fieldsvwomen who strengthened their mental capacity and mastered their bodies in ways few of us may ever accomplish. Working with them reminded me of how crushing abuse can be on the psyche of even the strongest people.

"I certainly didn't think it could happen to me. And I sure thought I understood how to effectively and calmly navigate the legal process."

It wasn't until I reached Harvard that I personally realized how trauma can result from feeling victimized, regardless of your physical or inner strength. I thought I understood how to handle people who abused me. I certainly didn't think it could happen to me. And I sure thought I understood how to effectively and calmly navigate the legal process.

As I advanced from attorney to chief operating officer to

chief legal officer, and shortly before becoming president of my firm, I wanted to further my education in business. I got accepted into Harvard Business School's prestigious Advanced Management Program, a graduate executive program designed specifically for upper-level professionals. It was a remarkable opportunity. The first section was taught by Harvard's stellar faculty in a virtual interactive classroom. The latter section was an intensive five weeks of on-campus, back-to-back classes, group sessions, and negotiations six days per week. One of the key values of the Advanced Management Program is building lifelong relationships with a brilliant group of classmates, so the program made room and opportunity for social interaction. We were organized into "living groups," which comprised students from all over the globe following a similar focus. We shared meals and housed in a common hall with private rooms. Only executives in the top tier of their company's leadership gained admission. We were all accomplished, trusted, and highly respected in our field.

When the virtual module was complete, I drove to Boston to attend the on-campus module. The first week flew by, but not without constant hard work. The program had us engaged from the moment we awoke until late into the evening. By Friday, we finally had a chance to wind down, and I was amazed. Here I was studying at Harvard, dining, laughing, and talking with my new colleagues, each of us successful in our fields, each of us smart and ambitious, and many of us, I suspect, concealing a nagging insecurity. *Did we really belong?*

On this night, I didn't question for a moment whether I belonged. We were pumped from the fun and intellectual vigor of the week. During our decadent dinner we indulged in a debate over the finer details of global economics, corporate responsibility in a digital world, and how to leverage strategic advantage in a competitive marketplace. It went so well that we carried it to our shared living space where the topics grew lighter and more playful. We laughed, we danced, we sang. At some point in the evening, I was sitting with George and Ben, both members of my living group, when George made a shocking confession.

"There's one woman in the program who makes my dick twitch!"

Up until then I'd viewed George as a quiet but seasoned executive. He followed his crude confession with howls of laughter before he prodded Ben to confess the same. "Come on, Ben. Admit it. There's got to be someone here you want."

Ben wasn't having it. He told George he loved his wife and changed the subject.

The vulgar comment had shifted the mood. I didn't like it. I thought about the unnamed woman and wondered whether she knew. Did she realize he thought—and now talked—about her that way when he saw her in class? Whenever she contributed to our class discussions, was he thinking about his dick? It never crossed my mind that the woman he was referring to was me.

Not long after George made his confession, I called it a night. It was late and though it was a Friday night, we had morning classes scheduled. As I walked down the hall to my room, I noticed George following me but didn't think much of it. I assumed he was heading to his room just two doors down. When I reached my door, instead of walking past me and wishing me good night, he stopped and, in an instant, he was standing just inches from me.

"Let's go in," he said quietly. Initially I thought this was his way of saying, "It's late. Good night." Room key in hand, I realized at first slowly and then with a start that he meant he wanted to come into *my* room, an interpretation that became clear as he continued standing so uncomfortably close that I could smell him.

Before I could respond, he grabbed my arm and pulled me towards him.

"I've been married for more than thirty years," he started, "but in all my life I've never felt this way about anyone."

I was stunned.

I barely knew him.

In the time since we'd met I thought of him as an older mentor-type man, and certainly nothing sexual. My one inclination in that moment was to get free of his grip. I struggled to break away, but he only grasped harder, and his face became deadly serious. So, I did what women learn to do in these situations. I tried to brush it off, to make light of it.

"Oh, that's so sweet, George," I said, "but I don't feel that way about you."

I tugged at my arm again but he wouldn't let go. Instead, he pulled me closer.

"Please," he begged, "just kiss me."

Still attempting to make light of the situation, I reached up and kissed him on the cheek while gently but firmly pushing him away with my free hand.

"That's all this will be, George," I told him. "I don't think of you in the same way."

I was certain that would end it, that we would part ways and he would be embarrassed the next day if he remembered it at all, and the drama would blow over.

I was wrong.

He grabbed my face, demanding I kiss him.

"Stop! Stop it, George," I protested, no longer making light of the situation. When I tried to wiggle free he became more aggressive. I repeated for him to stop, all the while thinking someone would come into the hallway and see what was going on, but no one did. I fumbled with my room key as I moved my head back and forth to escape his groping mouth. As I reached for the door handle he pulled my arm to stop me. It was in that instant that I realized I couldn't open the door. If I did, he would force his way into my room, and then no one could see us, and no one could stop him.

Repeatedly I told him to stop but he only grew bolder and more angry as I dodged his mouth. I pressed my hand against his chest again hoping he'd get the "stop" motion, but he did not. He held me fixed in place and refused to let go. Eventually —I'm not sure if it was twenty seconds or twenty minutes—he released his grip and headed to his room. I slipped into my own room and bolted it shut.

My heart raced. Memories of being held down flashed through my mind. As a child, an adult relative had repeatedly sexually abused me. Now fully grown, I couldn't bear to be held against my will. I was safe in my own room, but I could still feel his fingers pressing into my flesh. Minutes later my phone pinged. It was a text from George, and not to apologize.

"Beer?" he asked, as if I'd just brush everything aside, ignore the fact that he just tried to force himself on me, and join him for a drink.

The next morning I noticed bruises on my arm. Gazing at the darkening marks, I was no longer afraid. I was angry. *How dare he do that to me? Who the hell does he think he is?* I wondered what was it about me that made him think I was an easy target. In his mind we clearly weren't equals. I was subordinate.

I didn't go to classes that morning. Instead, I was glad that I could live-stream them from my room. I needed to be alone to process and didn't want to involve my classmates in the drama.

It was hard to concentrate. All I could do was keep reliving that moment. *Why didn't he stop? Was I not firm enough? Did I give him mixed messages? I should never have kissed him on the cheek.* I thought the kiss would clarify how I felt and mark an end to the encounter, not encourage him.

How many times had I told him to stop, or tried to push him away? How many times had he pushed himself further into my space against my body, grabbing me, holding me firmly in place, trying to force his mouth on me? My anger mounted. He had no right to do that. He disrespected me. He frightened me. He violated me.

"It was hard to concentrate. All I could do was keep reliving that moment."

By that afternoon I decided to confront him. I wanted him to know how I felt and that what he'd done was not okay. I sent him a text asking him to meet me outside in a public space and he immediately agreed.

Ten minutes later we were sitting at an outdoor table in front of our building where several men were building a pavilion. He wouldn't touch me there because he knew he had no right. He only grabbed me when no one was looking, when he thought he could get away with it. Outside, in full view of others, I was safe.

I told him that what he'd done was not at all okay. I reminded him of how many times I said no and how he'd ignored me. I told him that he'd disrespected me as a human being by putting his hands on me and making those aggressive advances after I'd clearly said no multiple times. George admitted I was right and confessed that he was wrong. He said he felt terrible about it, that he was embarrassed and was also hoping we could talk. In response, I asserted that he disrespected me as a professional and as a colleague in our graduate program. He nodded, his head low, mumbling his apologies. I showed him my arm. The red marks were turning to bruises.

"This is what you did to me. This is how hard you were gripping me," I told him.

He looked ashamed and apologized, blaming it on tequila.

"It wasn't the tequila," I told him. "It was you. You will never disrespect me in this way again, and if you ever again try to put your hands on me, you'll be sorry." My face was as firm as it had been the night before in all but one respect—this time, I wasn't afraid.

"I understand," he said. "Thank you for handling it in such a mature way."

I thought that in delivering my strength to him, in telling him how I truly felt, that I'd be done with it and the whole matter put to an end; but it didn't feel ended. I still felt stripped. I felt stripped of my power, autonomy, and self-respect. His shame-faced apologies didn't make me feel better. If anything, they made me angrier. His words of apology were those of a victim. He sounded more like a naughty boy who'd been caught stealing candy, unashamed of the act and only sorry that he got caught. The more he apologized, and the more he admitted that what he'd done to me was wrong, the more diminished, silenced, and shamed I felt.

"I wanted to say these things to you because you need to hear them directly," I heard myself say. "There are many other avenues I could have chosen, and I still may."

> *"I felt stripped of my power, autonomy, and self-respect."*

As he apologized yet again, he slowly raised his head and when he did, the penitent little boy was gone and the angry man had returned, his anger barely concealed by the cold glare and false smile stretched across his face. "I can assure you, Rebecca," he said eerily, "that it will never happen again."

My years of litigation on behalf of the injured and abused taught me that his expression meant that if I uttered a word, or if he even suspected I would talk, he would attempt to sow doubt about my character among our classmates.

The patterns of a quiet character assassination are unmistakable once you've seen them. It begins with small acts, dropped hints, innuendos. It's nuanced. Doubt is seeded with such a subtlety that no one even notices the manipulation. There are a thousand iterations, but the message always comes down to this: don't trust what she tells you. Most times, the victim never even knows the hints and comments were dropped. She just finds herself alone.

After George left, I spoke with a trusted friend from home who gave me strong advice to let someone else in my group know what had happened. That seemed like a good idea. I knew that people who keep silent can end up abused again and that their silence will be used against them if they eventually do speak up. There was no telling what George would do if he believed I wronged him by speaking up—and I wanted to have a witness. I thought of Ben and how he'd responded to George the night before, so I decided to approach him. Ben seemed to be a standup guy. After asking whether I could share something that had happened the night before and he agreed, I showed him the bruises on my arm and told him the whole story.

Ben was alarmed by the bruising and put into words what I hadn't yet articulated. "You've been assaulted," he said. "You should report this."

Trying to dismiss it, I assured him I was fine. I told him I'd already addressed George directly and didn't want to create more tension or make a big issue for the rest of the group. I let him know I just wanted someone to be aware of what had happened, just in case.

He offered his support and I thanked him, assuring him I'd be okay.

I wasn't okay. I stayed in my room all weekend and didn't join the group for our scheduled campus tour later that day or for dinner that night, and I spent most of Sunday in my room. I just couldn't bear to see George and I knew if I did, I wouldn't be able to concentrate. Just thinking about being in the same room with him sent anxiety all through me. So, I stayed in my room and fumed at what he'd done or, more accurately, what he *could* have done. What would have happened if I'd opened my door? If he would do that to me in a public hallway, what would he have done to me behind closed doors?

I fumed at how powerless I felt as he held me in his grip while I repeatedly said no, repeatedly dodged his mouth, repeatedly pushed him away. Nothing I said or did mattered. I had no power to say no. Everything was up to him from the moment he closed in on me and said, "Let's go inside," to the moment he'd walked away. He chose to be forceful. I chose to be polite. In the face of his aggression, I chose to be polite! Now that it was all over, my choice seemed absurd. I was mad at myself for not clocking him in the face or kicking him in the nuts when he wouldn't let go. For all his force, I felt like I couldn't respond with force, so I froze. It was that sense of powerlessness, of having no choice, that made me all the more determined to find my power.

I didn't see him again until our Monday morning group session where he showed up and acted as if nothing had happened. I continued to see him in classes throughout the day. I noticed rather than focusing on our professors, George remained turned toward me, openly glaring at me throughout the class. His body language felt like a direct challenge. I was uneasy the whole time. Even in the group I felt untrusting, wondering whether he'd said anything, or whether there were other guys in the group just like him. These were my new friends, but now I felt somehow like I wasn't one of them. I'd been set apart, singled out for assault. It didn't matter if he said nothing. What mattered was that I had been threatened and that threat didn't go away. If anything, the threat felt even greater. As for George, he was acting like nothing happened, just the same old happy guy.

By our third class that Monday I was in tears—and if you know me, you know this doesn't often happen. But as our professor expressed that our living group was now our "lifelong personal board of directors" and "trusted advisors for life," I broke. All I could think was that I'd miss out. I wouldn't be a part of that "personal board of directors" or have those "trusted advisors for life" because in just three short days, the walls I'd erected and the distance that had grown between me and my group had become too great. I thought I could handle it from there without reporting the incident and causing a commotion, but I never anticipated how the fear I felt that night would stay with me, growing greater by the hour, returning in waves every time I thought it had finally been washed away. The fear and PTSD I suffered from childhood abuse had returned with a powerful force. In all my personal injury and medical malpractice cases my clients had been grievously injured, their spouses killed, their babies died, or they had suffered lifelong disabilities due to someone else's actions or inactions. In those cases the sense of being wronged was theirs, not mine. I was the advocate, not the victim. I'd been the strong one, the fearless one, but now I was afraid. Now I was the one who'd been wronged, and though it was nothing compared to what they had been through, it was harder than I could have imagined.

After class I went to the bathroom in Tata Hall where a sign on the door provided a hotline to report sexual harassment.

"If you are a student who has experienced or witnessed sexual harassment including sexual assault, rape, relationship violence, or stalking—you don't have to go through it alone. Call for support and to review your options—anonymous calls are welcomed."

The sign went on to explain that crisis counseling, information about reporting, referrals to on- and off-campus resources, and other services would be provided. I wrote the number down and then went for a walk alone. Taking in the aromatic spring air, I sat down on a concrete wall in front of the iconic Baker Library overlooking the Charles River, pulled out my phone, and dialed the number. I had no idea how calling that number would wind up teaching me more about the ugly process of coming forward than any book or law class ever had. My education had just begun.

CHAPTER 3

THE FIRST STEP: A TRAUMA-INFORMED RESPONSE

Virtually every lawsuit a plaintiff brings against an institution alleging preventable or foreseeable injury begins with a formal or informal report. Once it is filed, someone in an official capacity evaluates the claimant's credibility and the merits of their claim. The evaluator either:

1. Believes the report, with or without some questions, and then takes action to address the complaint.
2. Disbelieves the report, and then communicates that doubt to others up the pipeline.
3. Believes the report and takes efforts to quash further investigation to prevent a lawsuit.

This last response inevitably leads to the greatest damages. It's the "cover-up" that snowballs. We saw this at MSU with Larry Nassar and with a similar cover-up at Penn State that led to the university's public disgrace when the crimes of Jerry Sandusky came to light. When the horrifying spinal surgeries performed by Dr. Christopher Duntsch in Texas first aroused suspicions of egregious malpractice, no one took action. Even after surgeons and nurses reported their concerns, hospitals simply dismissed rather than report him, thus enabling him to continue carving up the spines of unsuspecting patients. When patients under the care of nurse Charles Cullen repeatedly died suspiciously, numerous reports by patients and staff were swept under the rug. The serial-killing nurse was quietly dismissed only to kill again at other hospitals.

The fear of litigation is a dangerous trend. When organizations treat red flag reports as threats to their reputation and finances rather than opportunities to take swift action, people are hurt—sometimes irrevocably. Many of Larry Nassar's victims were yet unborn when the first reports of abuse were made against him. Hundreds of victims could have been spared. Had the institutions taken the proper steps, none of these cases would have risen to the level of international scandal with executives leaving or forced into early retirement.

"The fear of litigation is a dangerous trend."

So what about the more common reports? At first, the person coming forward might not seem all that upset, so the report is either taken lightly and treated as a formality, or it's dismissed altogether. After all, if the incident really occurred the way the individual claimed, how are they so well composed? When the claimant later becomes outraged and demands action, their early composure is interpreted as evidence that the incident was minor, and the person is now exaggerating.

Conversely, the complainant might initially appear inconsolable, crying, raging, shaking in anger or fear as they demand that something be done. Such behavior could easily be construed as mental instability. They may be trying too hard to be convincing. Their reaction might be too dramatic, or their grief could be blinding them to the facts. It may be that their baby died but the incident had nothing to do with malpractice. Of course, in the face of tragedy the person may not be thinking clearly or responding appropriately.

Whatever the reason, when cases are not taken seriously they can rapidly escalate from rectifiable problems to full-scale lawsuits battled in the public eye through mainstream and social media. These are the cases that destroy reputations. They demand untold hours of time devoted to gathering evidence, interviewing witnesses, attending depositions, and even going to trial . . . and it all starts with the initial report. Too often, the person reviewing that report has no understanding of trauma's impact on the human brain so that, from the outset, things are perfectly staged to go wrong. Let's first consider the institutional reporting process, and then we'll look at how trauma fits into the picture.

SEEING THE PROCESS THROUGH THEIR EYES

The institutional process for responding to complaints is generally articulated through a series of policies and practices that involve multiple levels of administration. It might begin with an administrator or supervisor, or go straight to risk management, corporate leadership, equity and diversity offices, human resources, legal, or any number of other departments.

From the organization's perspective, the process is clear and typically looks something like this:

- Someone makes an accusation or raises a concern to an administrator.
- The administrator determines whether the claim merits action.
- The administrator then discusses the complaint with other administrators or formally sends the individual to another level of administration.
- If deemed necessary, the matter is reported for investigation and possibly to law enforcement.

If the claim is considered a serious one, it is usually sent to an investigative panel. Parties to the complaint are interviewed, witnesses are contacted, and evidence gathered. If the complaint is found to have merit, action may or may not be taken against the party charged with wrongdoing such as removal from the group or organization. From their end the process is clear and, if not simple, at least as fair and as streamlined as possible.

"Taking that initial step of making a report can be frightening and downright humiliating . . . "

To those making the complaint, however, the process is anything but clear. Proving an incident that may have happened behind closed doors is inherently difficult. Explaining a situation that involves specialized areas of expertise such as in medical malpractice can be a significant challenge or downright confusing. The claimant also knows that making a serious allegation can get someone fired or even charged with a crime. Taking that initial step of making a report can be frightening and downright humiliating, especially if the alleged act includes sexual misconduct. A person who has been sexually assaulted comes to the process already violated, vulnerable, and shamed. They know they will be asked intimate, embarrassing questions. They know they will be doubted. They know that, in most cases, the only evidence they have is their own word. In a case of medical malpractice, the trusted nurse or doctor may have given them the wrong medication; left hardware, sponges, or bone fragments in their bodies during surgery; or failed to correctly deliver an infant in distress. They know that reporting means jeopardizing that relationship, threatening someone's career, and trying to make sense of a bewildering set of facts they may not fully understand.

For those reasons, someone who has been abused, injured, or otherwise harmed usually reports the incident informally. Just as I did, they may want a witness. They may want advice or just to be heard. So they talk to someone other than an administrator. Many are hoping that this first step will be all that is necessary. They hope to "nip it in the bud" by telling another human and garnering their support. Then, they may be thinking, if anything further happens *someone* knows and they may be able to offer support if needed.

Often, the person they speak to not only legitimates concerns but advises them to take further action to protect themselves, other potential victims, and the institution. As more people become involved in the process, trauma often begins to escalate as layers upon layers of individuals, panels, and committees enter the scene. Investigators and sometimes even peers begin to question, interrogate, doubt and, in some cases, directly or indirectly threaten them. All of this can lead to reputational damage, psychological trauma, and social abuse or shunning.

"Many are hoping that this first step will be all that is necessary."

The key takeaway is that the process of reporting wrongdoing feels and looks very different for the complainant than it does for those hearing and investigating the complaint. This distinction forms the underlying basis of this book and pinpoints why you need to learn how to protect your institution by better understanding the experience of those who bring you bad news.

UNDERSTANDING THE TRAUMATIZED BRAIN

No one really knows how they will respond to an injury or assault until it happens. Like me, one may think otherwise but discover they're unprepared for how the brain and body will process the incident. In my case, I had been sexually abused as a child. Being grabbed and confined by a sexually aggressive man triggered and heightened a latent fear of being held against my will. Many women who have survived childhood sexual abuse learn to shut down their emotions. Such women might relay the details of a violent rape in a deadpan voice with no more emotion than if they were giving directions to a grocery store, focusing plainly on the facts. Others might respond with a full-scale panic attack.

The same is true for any upsetting injury. The brain does its best to protect us from trauma by changing its neural circuitry. In the case of a traumatic event, it may heighten your awareness or sensitivity to anything that reminds you of the incident. This brain circuitry prepares us for "fight or flight" when faced with a perceived threat to our survival.

The amygdala is a part of the brain that processes emotion and memory. When our senses perceive a threat, the amygdala sends a signal to the hypothalamus, which controls our cells, organs, and hormones.[i]

"... the process of reporting wrongdoing feels and looks very different for the complainant than it does for those hearing and investigating the complaint."

The adrenal glands then flood our bodies with adrenaline; the liver produces extra glucose to provide energy; and our breathing and heart rate accelerate to prepare us for fight or flight. The brain's goal at this point is to shut down all unnecessary energy expenditures so that available energy can be used to

---

[i]   Zatev, Vadim et al. (2018), "Real-Time fMRI Neurofeedback Training of the Amygdala Activity with Simultaneous EEG in Veterans with Combat-Related PTSD," Science Direct, 18:106-121.

escape or destroy the threat. The digestive system slows, blood vessels constrict, and we stop producing saliva. Hearing and sight may shut down to silence extraneous noise and block out images from our periphery, giving us "tunnel vision." These are some of the actions of a brain in survival mode when we feel physically or emotionally threatened.[ii]

A grief response can also kick in. We tend to think of grief as a response to death and, in many cases of personal injury, that's exactly what's going on. However, grief is a response to any loss, whether of health, a body part, personal mobility, or a sense of security. Any time we feel we have lost something or someone central to our survival, stability, or identity, we grieve that loss. What's more, grief comes in stages that don't always follow a predictable sequence. The most common conception of this process, popularized by Dr. Elizabeth Kübler Ross,[iii,iv] is this patterned response:

1. **Shock or Denial:** The brain is unable to process what's happening. *It can't be real; it's just a misunderstanding;' it's not as bad as it appears.* If a report is made early enough, the claimant may still be in this stage, appearing logical and unaffected. They may make statements like, "It's no big deal," or "I just want a paper trail." In this case, emotions at the time of reporting are not a helpful gauge for the seriousness of the complaint. If you encounter a complainant in this stage of grief, it's important not to

---

ii Zhu, Xi, et al. (2022), "Sequential Fear Generalization and Network Connectivity in Trauma Exposed Humans With and Without Psychopathology," Communications Biology, 5:1275.
iii Kubler-Ross, Elizabeth (1969), *On Death and Dying*, Simon and Schuster.
iv Bremner, J. Douglas (2006), "Traumatic Stress: Effects on the Brain," Dialogues in Clinical Neuroscience, 8(4): 445-461.

take the matter too lightly because as subsequent stages kick in, their emotional reactions will change.

2. **Anger:** *This never should have happened. Someone or something caused my suffering.* If in this stage while making a report, the claimant will appear frightening, even threatening. They may blame the organization for something that was no one's fault, or their anger may be justified because someone or something was at fault. At this stage, arguing is not helpful. <u>This is the stage where it's most important for the person to be heard and their loss acknowledged.</u>

3. **Bargaining:** Whether it's making a deal with God (or any higher power) or with the organization, at this stage, the person is willing to do anything to undo the damage. They may pray that God takes them instead of the child they have lost. They may plead with the organization to just admit the mistake, just make it right. They want to see someone else do something to mitigate the damage and alleviate their pain. <u>This is often the stage where resolving the problem is most possible—you may not be able to undo the damage, but you may be able to prevent the damage from escalating.</u>

4. **Depression:** At this stage, reality has hit home. They realize they've lost something they won't regain, or they accept that they were abused and can't turn back time. They feel defeated, deprived, or cast aside by God, the universe, society, or an individual. They may have a flat affect, showing no emotion; or they may appear extremely sad. Some may even be catatonic, not responding at all. <u>This state usually passes, or it may last a long time.</u>

5. **Acceptance:** Acceptance is always the final stage, regardless of the order in which the previous stages

were presented. By this stage, the person accepts his or her loss and is ready to move on with life. <u>This doesn't mean they are ready to accept a settlement or drop a lawsuit if they've initiated one, especially if they feel they've been abused by the process during these earlier stages</u>, but it does mean that they accept what has happened.

"The trauma response is complex. It can permanently change our brains . . . "

As you can see, someone making a report of loss or injury might be presenting at any one of these stages, and how they appear may have more to do with how their brain is processing information than how the incident has or will impact them eventually. What's more, grief isn't all that's affecting how they present. The trauma response is complex. It can permanently change our brains as the neural pathways disconnect and reconnect to forge new circuits. Think of a train switching tracks and heading in a new direction to avoid an unsafe destination. This is a picture of the traumatized brain as it determines a course of action.

MISREADING THE CUES, MISLEADING CONCLUSIONS

What we once termed "shell shock" to explain the behaviors and cognitive changes in soldiers returning from battle we now understand as Post-Traumatic Stress Disorder or PTSD. You've undoubtedly heard the term many times. If you haven't experienced it yourself, the behaviors someone displays following a traumatic event may appear to be maladaptive at best and downright crazy at worst. That's because as the amygdala and hypothalamus get busy with the fight-or-flight response, other parts of the brain and body get in on the action, as well. In the initial moments of a threat, adrenal glands flood the body with adrenaline while the pituitary gland produces cortisol, heightening the alert system. This physiological response explains the hyper vigilance often seen in people with PTSD as they react to sudden sounds, movements, or perceived threats, or when they startle easily and scan their environments for indication of a threat.

"The most influential factor in how the administrator perceives and responds to the claim is the trauma response itself."

Once this fight-or-flight response is triggered, it can be difficult to shut off even after the threat has passed. The person might even appear calmer, but the body continues to produce high levels of these stress hormones, which in turn affect perception of the environment. One stimulus triggers a thought that may trigger a cascade of thoughts that trigger an emotion that triggers a behavior—and the brain's neural pathways get stuck.

It's for this reason that someone who has experienced a traumatic event may seem unable to "move on" from it. Neurons can be damaged and even die over time, and neurogenesis, the ability to form new neurons and process new information, can be inhibited. Then may come recurrent memories of the event, nightmares, or obsessive thinking about what happened, which can continue throughout the healing process. To stop the unrelenting pain of PTSD, many people self-medicate through drugs, alcohol, or other addictions such as computer addiction. They are trying to shut off the neural circuitry.

This means that neither the claimant's credibility nor even the nature of the event itself may be the primary influence upon the administrator's evaluation. <u>The most influential factor in how the administrator perceives and responds to the claim is the trauma response itself.</u> The administrator may be taking cues by "reading" the person, thus being misled depending on the person's handle on their emotions and where they are in the stages of grief and healing from trauma. The way the administrator receives the report can pave the way for how the matter is handled as it moves up the pipeline. Especially if doubtful or aggressive, the nature of their response invariably circles back to impact the trauma response itself. In other words, you can trigger the person to a heightened response and miss the truth as well as the opportunity to alleviate suffering because you've failed to address what really matters in that early stage. Instead of a compassionate, humane response, a disinterested or even adversarial reaction is likely to clash with the already alarmed, traumatized state of the complainant. This can rapidly escalate conflicts and multiply misunderstandings between the claimant and the institution all because of a failure to understand how trauma sets in and plays out over time.

Employ a trauma-informed response from the outset. This is the key to bridging the divide between these two reporting experiences, and it is the first step to an on-target response. That means you understand how trauma might affect how someone is presenting the information to you, or how they are communicating or acting in general.

TRAUMA-INFORMED RESPONSE

When someone reports a bad outcome from a birth gone wrong, a death on a construction site, or an assault by a trusted caregiver, it's understandable that the first instinct might be that they're mistaken. If the person is angry or accusatory, it's understandable to want to counter defensively. If they are screaming or rambling incoherently, it's understandable to question whether they are mentally unstable. If they are talking monotone with no sign of stress or emotion, it's understandable to think the issue isn't a big deal.

"In the rare case the claimant is lying, their comfort with you will only bring that forward more quickly as they become more emboldened in their storytelling."

However, in almost all cases, by the time someone makes a formal report of wrongdoing, something has happened to leave them emotionally shaken. Often, their inability to articulate the incident in a way you find coherent makes them appear overreactive or nonreactive and their claim seem weak.

A trauma-informed response begins with the assumption that the person has been traumatized. This assumption might fly in the face of what you have been taught. Good institutional practices probably don't place compassion and understanding at the top of their list for responding to complaints. In fact, these typically don't make the list at all, but when you start in this way you build trust. That trust tells the traumatized individual that it's safe to let their guard down, at least a little. Seeing you care enough to understand helps the person open up and reveal what happened as they experienced it. In the rare case the claimant is lying, their comfort with you will only bring that forward more quickly as they become more emboldened in their storytelling. However, in the more likely case that they at least believe their claim has merit, your trauma-informed response will ease their defenses, which will greatly impact their ability to handle the next steps.

"By starting with the assumption that the person was traumatized, you open the door for disclosure."

Providing a trauma-informed response does not mean the investigation is over or the findings determined before you've begun. It means you start with understanding that something has happened to traumatize the person who has come to you with a report. What that something is, how it happened, why it happened, who was involved, what kind of injury was sustained, if any, and whether it was coercive, forced, or with some form of consent given, are all matters for the investigation.

By starting with the assumption that the person was traumatized, you open the door for disclosure.

Trauma-informed care emerged from the healthcare and social services professions where professionals found themselves on the frontlines of treating rape victims. As I'll show, if the process escalates their trauma, you might face higher damages. It may not be in your job description to help the parties to heal, but you are a pivotal figure in the trajectory of how the situation unfolds throughout your institutional processes.

Let's consider the five basic principles of trauma-informed care. Your job is not to provide care, but the same principles that guide caretakers can help you to provide an effective response during the initial report. Responding in line with the principles of trauma-informed care, you will likely defuse many potential points of conflict and make the process easier for everyone involved. These principles are:

1. **Bear witness to their experience of trauma.** Begin by assuming they've been traumatized. Serve as a witness as they relate their experience.

2. **Help them feel safe.** Provide them a safe space to talk, both physically and psychologically. This is no time for an interrogation or cross-examination. You will have plenty of time to ask probing questions, but with the initial report you want them to feel safe and believed. Listen without showing judgment. Help them relax and tell you what they want you to know.

3. **Include them in the process.** In many cases you can avoid nasty lawsuits just by openly communicating, asking the claimant what they want and need, and helping them feel they are engaged in the process rather than an annoyance or a problem.

4. **Trust in their strength and resilience.** When someone has been injured or suffered a grievous loss they will not usually appear strong and resilient. If the ensuing process is fair, safe, and engages the one(s) making the report, they will grow stronger. If it is accusatory, biased, and excludes them as much as possible, they will be weakened. Trust that given the right treatment from you they'll be strong and resilient and your job will be easier.

5. **Respect cultural, gender, class, and age differences.** Many women preface their statements with qualifications such as: *"Maybe," "I think," "Do you think," "How about,"* or *"I may be wrong but . . . "* That doesn't mean they aren't certain of what they experienced. Some people are more likely to speak directly and view anger as a strength. They may sound threatening when they are trying to display confidence. Others may be more emotionally restrained. That doesn't mean they weren't profoundly impacted.

"Being sensitive to trauma responses can make or break the investigative process."

Being sensitive to trauma responses can make or break the investigative process. By reforming the investigative process from a defensive one that sets out to disprove the claim to a trauma-informed response through every stage of the process, you increase the chances that those making reports feel heard. As a result:

- You will be less likely to be sued.
- Your perceived sensitivity is likely to mitigate damages.
- The conflict is less likely to play out in the press.
- You're more likely to identify those in the organization who most threaten you—not by reporting but by *causing* the problems that prompt the reports.
- Your organizational culture is likely to have a higher morale because there will be less fear, less secrecy, and fewer rumors swirling around.
- The process itself is likely to be less exhausting and draining for everyone involved.

HOW TO PUT IT INTO PLACE

You might be wondering what it's going to take to introduce a trauma-informed approach into your institution. Fortunately, it isn't something that requires an overhaul of your mission statement or even a rewriting of your policies. What it takes is a shift in thinking. You shift from viewing the complaint as a problem to do away with, and instead see it as an opportunity to do away with potential threats to the safety and security of your institution.

You may feel conflicted upon hearing reports about someone in leadership or someone you like and respect. In those cases, you might feel inclined to dismiss the complaint because it's uncomfortable to launch an investigation into a person of power or social influence, or because the person accused is someone you consider a trusted friend. You might feel the accusation is wholly out of character based on what you know of the person. Be careful. Even if that is the case, first of all, everyone can make mistakes. Second, how someone acts among friends is not necessarily how they act around others with less power. Few could believe Larry Nassar or Bill Cosby were serial sexual predators because both men were friendly, engaging, and highly ethical in public and within their social circles. Yet, when alone with women in a vulnerable position, we saw another side of them.

"The trauma-informed approach sets everyone at ease."

If the person accused is a friend or has authority over you, you have a conflict of interest and someone else should be appointed to the investigation. Make every effort to distance yourself. If that is not possible, be careful not to let your relationship with that person bias your investigation or that bias can do great damage to you and your institution. It's tough, I know, but if you take the steps I present in the next chapters your sensitivity to the concerns of everyone involved will do more than improve your interactions as you conduct interviews. It will also protect you because you'll be less likely to come off as a threat even to those in power. The trauma-informed approach sets everyone at ease.

Larry Nassar was a big name in athletics not only at

Michigan State University, but with the U.S. Olympic gymnastics. Jerry Sandusky and Joe Paterno were national football legends. Not many people had heard of Charles Cullen, but he was considered an excellent nurse. Now that he's been convicted of serial killings his name is widely known. Dr. Christopher Duntsch was just like any other surgeon until his criminally botched surgeries left so many patients dead or paralyzed that he is now serving a life sentence in prison and has been called "Dr. Death." In every case, dozens or hundreds of young children, men, and women could have been spared from death or lifelong trauma. Moreover, the institutions involved would have suffered minimally had the reports of these abusers been taken seriously from the start. Billions of dollars could have been saved.

The purpose of the trauma-informed response is not to turn your investigations "touchy-feely" or give people free reign to vent their grievances over a compliment or off-color joke. The trauma-informed response fosters mutual understanding, respect, and a sense of safety so you can more effectively determine the truth, make the investigation less stressful, save you money, and safeguard your reputation without causing further injury. If that sounds like something that would benefit you, read on.

Next, we'll discuss what is at the heart of every report—he said/she said, or as I like to call it, history v. herstory. You'll learn ways you can better assess and reconcile competing narratives to protect everyone's rights, get to the truth, and safeguard the institution.

CHAPTER 4

UNRAVELING THE FACTS

Coming forward is not easy. In fact, it can be terrifying because coming forward means risking retaliation, harassment, or even false claims against the plaintiff. After all, a settlement can be drastically reduced if a defendant can prove contributory negligence. The entire claim can be defeated if a plaintiff is viewed by a jury or the court as lacking credibility. That's why defendants scour our clients' social media looking for ammunition they can use against them. A picture of the client smiling for a brief moment at a family function can turn into a storyline about the person faking their hardship, as if you are never allowed to smile once you've suffered an injury. Experience has also taught me that the complexities of a case can obscure even the most seemingly clear set of facts. I thought I knew what I was up against when I made that initial call, but I was wholly unprepared for the powerful emotional impact of coming forward.

A woman answered the phone. I told her I was a student and wanted to discuss a sexual assault.

"What program are you in?" she asked.

"I'm in the Advanced Management Program."

"I'm afraid I can't help you," she replied, dismissing me. "This number is for MBA students, not the exec program."

Then why, I wondered, *did they post the number in the building where all my classes were held and where we lived? Was there a different number to call for every department on campus?* I asked her for the correct number. She didn't know but offered to "try and find" some campus resources.

I didn't want resources. I wanted to talk with someone. I wanted to be heard.

I hung up feeling lost and alone. What I needed was support —someone to hear me, to assure me that I was safe. This roadblock set in motion my sense of defeat from the start.

"I didn't want resources. I wanted to talk with someone. I wanted to be heard."

The night when George assaulted me I was terrified to open my door in fear he'd push his way in, but it was the intensifying revulsion and creeping fear that he'd return that kept my nerves on edge long past the night. I thought when I'd finally gotten into my room and bolted the door that I'd feel safe, but as the days passed the uncertainty of what he'd do next continued to plague my thoughts. He'd already shown me his dark side, a determination to take what he wanted. I'd drawn the line, but was he going to show me he could and would cross it? What's more, I knew that aggressors don't just one day turn aggressive. He'd no doubt done this before. He would no doubt do it again to some other woman and when he did, how far would he go?

These fears persisted as not only did he continue to watch me in class, making concentration all the more difficult, but every time I left my room to enter the common area, I felt my heart race as I scanned the area for him. The hallway was dark. The lights were motion sensitive and only dimly lit when movement was detected in the initially dark space. Just going for my 5 a.m. cup of coffee terrified me. I nearly ran to the common area. I feared him lurking in the shadows, waiting to grab me, determined to finish what he'd started. I didn't realize it at first, but my hyper vigilance was a symptom of PTSD and common to people who have been assaulted. What I normally would have perceived as no big deal—a guy making a pass—didn't feel that way this time. I'd had guys make passes at me before. They didn't leave bruises on my body. They didn't hold me against my will. They didn't scare me. George had scared me and I didn't feel safe living in the same building with him, sharing the same classes and common areas. I'd read the university's policies for student behavior: "Respect for the rights, differences, and dignity of others. Honesty and integrity in dealing with members of the community. Accountability for personal behavior." The policies further stated that in joining the Harvard Business School community, students agreed to abide by these standards of behavior. It was clear George had violated these standards.

Early Tuesday morning, four days after the assault, I emailed the program director: "Something happened Friday night that I need to discuss with you," I wrote. "I've thought very much about this and, after careful consideration, feel I have no option but to inform you."

She invited me to her office right away. I relayed the events of that night and expressed how frightened I remained.

"I don't know what to say," she said, shaking her head. "We've never had anything like this happen before."

Perhaps she was correct that nothing like that had been *reported*, but I knew that it couldn't be true that nothing like this had ever happened, just given the nature of university campuses. The fact is harassment—even in graduate executive programs—happens all the time.

She assured me that she was appalled, that she would take the matter seriously, and that she thought George would be removed from the program. She said she would have to contact several people including HR, a program administrator responsible for "community values," and a male and female faculty member. I left her office feeling heard and confident that they'd deal with George.

Later that morning after class I received a call and was asked to meet with the HR liaison to recount details of the incident. I did so and was told they would get back to me after relaying the matter to two more offices: the Office for Gender Equity (OGE) and the Office of General Counsel (OGC).

"Can I speak with them directly?" I asked.

As an attorney and a victim—a term I don't love for myself or anyone—it was important to me that the event be presented factually and not become distorted as others narrated it.

"You *can*," she said, her voice conveying that she did not like the idea, "but it might be better if I speak with them first and get back to you."

I agreed. I didn't want to make trouble. Unfortunately, I already had.

UNTANGLING COMPETING NARRATIVES

From the moment you take a report alleging someone has been harmed in some way connected to your organization, competing narratives can emerge and often rapidly evolve into competing narratives of victimization. A woman alleges that she was assaulted; the accused responds that he is a victim of false accusation. A patient alleges that a surgeon botched a surgical procedure; the surgeon alleges she has been wrongfully accused of malpractice. A driver alleges that his brakes failed causing him critical injuries; the automaker alleges false malignment claiming the real problem was the driver's neglect of his car. In each of these scenarios, the conflicting narratives damage reputations and your organization takes the hit. Your task is to minimize that damage for *everyone* involved. Why everyone?

> *"The fewer people who suffer damage—either from direct injury, emotional duress, or reputational damage—the less damage your organization will suffer."*

The fewer people who suffer damage—either from direct injury, emotional duress, or reputational damage—the less damage your organization will suffer. This was a lesson Oberlin College learned to the tune of nearly $40 million.

―――――

GIBSON BAKERY

In 2016, the owners of a local bakery that served the faculty, staff, and students at Oberlin College in Ohio found themselves the focus of a viral media campaign when a clerk called the police on three black Oberlin students. The clerk, grandson of the owner, had accused the three of attempted robbery and assault. The three countered with an accusation of racial profiling. Cries of racism erupted. Without proof or investigation, the community called for a ban of the restaurant. Even the college vice president and dean of students joined in the effort. They actively passed out fliers urging people to boycott Gibson Bakery and suggesting alternative places to do business.

Their efforts proved successful: the fifth-generation family business was forced to close. Meanwhile, the students in question pled guilty when video recordings showed they had indeed committed the offenses of which they were accused. They had not been targeted for their race, but for their actions.

Unfortunately, the damage was done. The bakery's reputation and business were destroyed. They took the college to court and won. The college was court ordered to pay $36.59 million in damages. Had administrators investigated the matter more objectively and not accepted the narrative that conformed to their preconceptions, they may have saved the college a great deal of money and reputational damage. Instead, they reacted by accepting a narrative that fit their beliefs without knowing the facts.

―――――

GOOD INTENTIONS, BAD OUTCOMES

It's important not to assume that you know the facts before they've been gathered regardless of your "hunches." Even along the way of gathering these facts, preconceptions and biases can shape how you proceed. Emotions play a powerful role in fact-finding, but if you're aware of that and can keep preconceived notions in check, you'll be more likely to come away with a fairly accurate understanding of what happened.

"In cases with merit, listening to what they want is key."

I'm not suggesting that every claim has merit. I recognize that there are people who threaten to sue at the slightest sense they've been wronged. So, how does one distinguish between cases with merit, some merit, and no merit?

The person who is just looking for a payout is likely to demand money right off the bat, showing little interest in understanding. They may have a history of litigation with few cases going to trial. These opportunists are generally easy to spot because they aren't interested in correcting the problem.

In cases with merit, listening to what they want is key. These claimants will express a range of emotions. While they may hint at suing, they are far more likely to want you to hear what happened and how it affected them. They may express anger or reject certain options, but their primary concern will be having someone acknowledge the problem, explain what happened, and express empathy with how the problem has impacted them. These are the claimants who are likely to be open to a range of solutions, at least in the early stages, and these are the ones you are best positioned to help. As you do try to help, keep in mind that if someone feels they have the moral high ground it can be difficult for them to see the facts objectively. This doesn't just mean the claimant. It can mean you, as well.

You can be blinded by good intentions and things can go terribly wrong. If you deem one person or group of people vulnerable and try to protect them, you might render yourself unable to objectively consider the evidence or take alternative narratives seriously. One tragic example of good intentions obscuring reasoned reflection is the case of Beata Kowalski and Johns Hopkins All Children's Hospital in St. Petersburg, Florida.[i]

> *"You can be blinded by good intentions and things can go terribly wrong."*

---

i   Hauser, Christine (2023), "Family in 'Take Care of Maya' Documentary is Awarded $261 Million," *New York Times*, November 10, available online at: 'Take Care of Maya' Family Awarded $261 Million in Court - The New York Times (nytimes.com).

CASE STUDY
JOHNS HOPKINS ALL CHILDREN'S HOSPITAL

In 2015, Beata and Jack Kowalski's then nine-year-old daughter, Maya, began exhibiting a series of debilitating symptoms. She had problems breathing, skin rashes and sores, severe pain, and a burning sensation in her feet. Any touch was excruciating. Eventually confined to a wheelchair and unable to walk, the Kowalskis consulted numerous doctors about their daughter's disorder, but physicians remained perplexed. Eventually, a specialist diagnosed Maya with a rare neurological disorder called Complex Regional Pain Syndrome (CRPS) and recommended an experimental treatment available in Mexico. The Kowalskis felt they had no choice but to try the procedure, which involved an induced coma for five days. While in the coma, Maya received high doses of the drug ketamine, commonly referred to as a "rape drug" for its ability to erase memory.

The treatment appeared to work. Maya returned home on a lower dose of ketamine infusions and her symptoms lessened considerably. Then in 2016, the symptoms returned with such severity that the Kowalskis rushed their daughter to the E.R. at the nearby Johns Hopkins All Children's Hospital. That's when everything went sideways.

Doctors immediately became suspicious of Beata when she, herself a nurse, insisted they not touch Maya and that Maya receive the high dose of ketamine. The attending physician believed Beata was deliberately dosing her daughter with the drug to knock her out and inflict injuries on her in an effort to gain the attention of physicians. Such acts are not unheard of. In fact, there is a specific mental health syndrome, Munchausen Syndrome by Proxy (MSP), to describe people who injure or sicken others, usually their children, for attention. The inexplicable injuries combined with the mother's insistence on the high dose of ketamine appeared to the attending physician as a classic case of

MSP. The county was contracted with a private social-welfare company to oversee cases of child abuse and neglect. The physician alerted the company and after one brief interview with Maya, the social worker recommended Maya be placed in the care of the State of Florida. A no-contact order was filed against Beata, Maya's mother, pending investigation into child abuse, and Beata was prohibited from all communications with her daughter.

Maya was told her mother was crazy and prevented from leaving or communicating with anyone outside the hospital for three months. No one was permitted to visit her, including friends, extended family and even teachers, thus leaving Maya with no educational instruction. Even her priest was barred from visiting. Eventually, monitored visits with Maya's father and brother were permitted. When Maya's condition did not improve, they concluded Maya herself was faking the disorder and the lesions on her skin were self-inflicted. [ii]

In the meantime, Beata complied with a court-ordered psychiatric evaluation, which concluded there was no evidence of MSP. Rather, the evaluator found that Beata was extremely agitated over her daughter's confinement and the fact that Maya was not getting the treatment the parents wanted for her. Indeed, Maya was not receiving treatment for CRPS, which hospital staff alleged she did not have as they accused her of lying about her symptoms.

Eventually, on January 6, 2017, the court denied Beata's motion to visit her daughter. When she asked if she could at least hug her in court, the judge ruled she could not. Beata returned home and hung herself. Five days later, Maya was released from Johns Hopkins and went home to her father and brother.

The family sued the hospital and the Pinellas County child protection team. The lawsuit caught the attention of a reporter for the **Sarasota Herald-Tribune** who found that several parents had experienced

---

ii Neary, Dyan (2023), "What Happened to Maya: When a 10-Year-Old Girl Complained of Mysterious Pain, a Doctor Suspected Child Abuse. How Far Would She Go to Prove It?" *New York Magazine*, November 9, Available online at: The True Story Behind 'Take Care of Maya' (thecut.com)

similar false accusations of abuse by the same medical director, Dr. Sally Smith.[iii] Moreover, although the hospital's position was that Maya did not have CRPS and they refused to treat her for it, records eventually proved they had submitted over 174 insurance claims for CRPS treatment of Maya.[iv] Maya alleged the overseer of her care, Cathi Bedy, had pinned her down and forcibly removed Maya's clothes to photograph her body. It turns out Cathi Bedy had previously been charged with child abuse. Not surprisingly, no one would speak to Maya's pediatrician who originally diagnosed her with CRPS. Had administrators at the hospital not been so blinded by their staff's preconceived ideas, they might have been spared a $261 million jury award and a Netflix series that did real damage to the hospital's reputation.

"Had administrators at the hospital not been so blinded by their staff's preconceived ideas, they might have been spared a $261 million jury award and a Netflix series that did real damage to the hospital's reputation."

[iii] Chen, Daphne and Nicole Rodriguez (2019), "Doctor's Suspicion Tears Apart Venice Family," *The Herald-Tribune*, January 27. Available online at: Doctor's suspicion tears apart Venice family (heraldtribune.com).

[iv] Neary, Dyan (2023), "What Happened to Maya: When a 10-Year-Old Girl Complained of Mysterious Pain, a Doctor Suspected Child Abuse. How Far Would She Go to Prove It?" *New York Magazine*, November 9, Available online at: The True Story Behind 'Take Care of Maya' (thecut.com).

The Netflix documentary about the case, *Take Care of Maya,* reveals that most people who lost custody of their children over abuse allegations and were later found to be innocent were unable to sue the hospital. This happened because they'd agreed to parenting plans compelling them to take anger management courses, get mental health treatment, or otherwise take steps to regain access to their children. The parents in the documentary just wanted to see their kids again. They'd hoped that their compliance would satisfy their accusers and restore their parental rights. Instead, their compliance was interpreted as admission of wrongdoing. One family, the Kowalskis, did not agree to do the parenting plan. The Kowalskis' willingness to at first be characterized as uncooperative ultimately enabled them to prevail in court, dealing a huge blow to the organization's finances and reputation.

WHAT SEEMS OBVIOUS CAN BE FAR FROM THE TRUTH

So what went wrong? How did the hospital and child protection facility begin with good intentions but wind up liable for such a high judgment? Bad went to worse turned to tragedy because they did not recognize Beata's behavior as consistent with someone being traumatized by the process.

Beata was an immigrant from Poland and English was not her first language. She was accustomed to being taken lightly by people in positions of authority and, thus, had developed an assertive personality that could make her appear abrasive. She was also a nurse and had studied Maya's condition in exhaustive detail. In her efforts to communicate that knowledge, she was perceived as interfering with Maya's care. She knew, as well, that any touch, even loud noises or bright lights could be excruciatingly painful for Maya, so she did not want them to touch Maya. Hospital staff perceived that as not wanting Maya to be examined or treated. Given these many misperceptions it's understandable that staff might think she was mentally unstable and potentially abusive. Had the matter ended at that point with an objective investigation, it is likely Maya would have been discharged early on, received the treatment she'd needed from her former pediatrician, and Beata would be alive today.

"No one seemed ever to consider the possibility that they were wrong."

That's not what happened.

What happened was that every effort Beata made to help or even see her daughter led to a response from staff to limit her maternal role. Beata reacted by becoming more angry, feeling more powerless, and trying to regain power by making phone calls, writing letters, documenting what was happening, and retaining attorneys. The more she tried to regain power, the more aggressive hospital staff became against her, and the more aggressive she became in response. Such escalating power battles and emotional flooding are common when someone feels unheard. In Beata's case, not only was she perceived as crazy, but recordings obtained through discovery revealed, as played on the Netflix documentary, that staff laughed at how their actions provoked her. Beata was mentally and physically exhausted due to many sleepless nights; the cost of treatments had forced the family to sell their home and file bankruptcy; and these were all considered efforts on Beata's part to draw attention to herself.

Potential witnesses who could counter the perception that Maya was abused were not interviewed, despite their efforts to be heard. Maya's pediatrician who had diagnosed the CRPS was ignored, and extended family members were considered biased. Only those witnesses who would corroborate the suspicion of abuse were interviewed.

Finally, Maya herself was abused by the hospital staff seeking to protect her. When her symptoms persisted despite isolation from family, they still failed to question their conclusions and presumed she was self-inflicting injuries and faking her pain. No one seemed ever to consider the possibility that they were wrong.

Beata Kowalski was overwhelmed by her daughter's illness and the financial impact the treatment had on their family, but when she sought help from Johns Hopkins she found herself under threat. According to the Netflix documentary, one doctor had warned her that Maya would die a slow and painful death without proper treatment. Beata was terrified her daughter would not get the treatment she needed. She was terrified Maya would get worse and that the state would never return Maya to her family. These were not paranoid delusions. They were very real threats she faced that caused her trauma while no one would listen.

The hospital staff and the child protection team no doubt believed they were doing their best to protect Maya. They no doubt had good intentions to identify and address suspected abuse, and no doubt had considerable experience with parents who really did abuse their children, but our good intentions can blind us to bad outcomes or prevent us from considering we might be wrong. As you can see, the institutional process of investigations and rulings can jeopardize a person's sense of security resulting in trauma, and that trauma can make them behave in crazy or even aggressive ways. When investigators don't recognize or understand trauma, they may then conclude with even greater certainty that they are right—even when they're wrong.

"When investigators don't recognize or understand trauma, they may then conclude with even greater certainty that they are right—even when they're wrong."

THE ROLE OF TRAUMA IN HOW FACTS ARE PRESENTED

When someone comes to you with a complaint, whether it is a personal injury, medical malpractice, sexual assault, or sexual harassment claim, your first instinct may be to question the validity of what they're saying. Your second thought is likely to be a quick assessment of whether the allegation has legs, i.e., whether you may end up battling the claimant in court or settling with a hefty sum of money. Somewhere in there you try to tease out the facts as you assess the claimant's credibility.

> *"It was his traumatic emotional response that put Russ Faria in prison for four years when he came home to discover his wife's blood-covered body on the living room floor."*

As you learned from the last chapter, however, the person making the claim may not be presenting the matter in the best frame of mind. They might seem over the top with emotion, sobbing, raging, or begging for help. Conversely, they might be so void of emotion that any claim of emotional distress or injury is hard to believe. What's important is to ensure that anyone taking an initial report of wrongdoing is able to provide a trauma-informed response and understands the range of emotional responses a grieving or traumatized person may present.

It was his traumatic emotional response that put Russ Faria

in prison for four years when he came home to discover his wife's blood-covered body on the living room floor.

―――――

CASE STUDY
A Widower Unjustly Jailed

Betsy Faria had been stabbed fifty-five times, but all Russ saw was the blood. Knowing his wife was distressed from a terminal diagnosis of cancer and in shock to see her in such a state, when he phoned police, he said she had committed suicide. In his traumatized state, he didn't see the knife wounds. Despite having an alibi backed by multiple witnesses, a fast-food receipt, and his purchase recorded on camera making it impossible for him to have committed the crime, Faria's implausible explanation of suicide followed by what officers felt were over-the-top displays of grief were enough to convince the officers of his guilt. They didn't bother looking into Betsy's friend, Pam Hupp, who just days before the killing had taken out a life insurance policy on the victim and was also the last person to see Betsy alive. Eventually, Pam killed again and got caught, leading to Faria's exoneration. The police department paid him a legal settlement of $2 million for their rush to judgment that blinded them to the evidence of Hupp's guilt from the start. As these officers discovered, failure to understand how trauma may prevent people from registering important details can lead to costly miscalculations.

―――――

"APPROPRIATE" RESPONSES TO TRAUMATIC EVENTS

One common assumption in assessing the credibility of a claim, particularly if it involves sexual assault or some other violent act, is that the victim "should have" escaped from the danger.

"Why didn't you leave?", "Why didn't you run?", or even "Why didn't you just say no?" are typical questions victims are asked when they report a sexual assault. One of the most recent and perplexing variations of this question arose regarding four college students in Idaho who were viciously murdered in their beds. The alleged killer, Bryan Kohberger, is on trial for their murders as I write this.

"When we are traumatized, we do not always act rationally or as we expect."

A roommate reported hearing someone cry, followed by a male voice saying that he was there to help. There was a loud thump. Then, in the dark of night, she saw a masked man walk through the house and leave through the sliding glass door. No one phoned the police for another seven hours.

"Why didn't she call the police?" came the public condemnation. Some even suggested she must have been involved in the murder to have gone back to her room without calling authorities.

Shock can take hours to subside. Humans don't consciously

choose fight or flight. Whether we fight back or freeze in terror is an auto response chosen by our primal limbic system—not our conscious minds.[v] While I cannot say why the roommate didn't call the police, or even what factually happened that tragic night in Idaho, it's possible that the roommate's shock and terror hijacked her brain and caused her to freeze or even shut out what she had seen. When we are traumatized, we do not always act rationally or as we expect. When George grabbed my arm firmly enough to leave bruises, I froze. As much as people think fear makes us fight back, that isn't always so. A condition known as "tonic immobility" can prevent a person from being able to physically move or cry out for help. We often hear stories of people being violently assaulted who could have gotten away or called for help, but they said or did nothing stating they were too terrified. That response might seem on the surface to make no sense, but in a state of trauma the unconscious brain is in charge. In the same way, when a traumatized victim tells their story, it may not seem to make sense.

"When interviewing traumatized victims, be careful not to presume they 'should' have acted in a manner that you feel would have been appropriate."

There's no way to know when a person's fear response will kick in. For someone previously traumatized, the fear might kick

---

[v]   The Neurobiology of trauma and interviewing victims.pdf

in quickly causing them to freeze or fight at the first trigger. For others, it may take longer to feel a sense of danger. <u>When interviewing traumatized victims, be careful not to presume they "should" have acted in a manner that you feel would have been appropriate.</u>

SELF-BLAME CAN MUDDY PERCEPTIONS

Complicating the way we often interpret the reactions of assault victims is the victim's own self-blame. Because perpetrators often groom their victims by establishing trust and even culpability on the part of the victim, when someone has been victimized by a predator, they don't always realize it. As social beings, our brains have evolved to create emotional attachments to other humans. By establishing trust with their victim, perpetrators activate this emotional attachment. Retired Sgt. Joanne Archambault with psychologists Christopher Wilson and Kimberly Lonsway prepared a report for the organization, End Violence Against Women International (EVAWI),[vi] in which they showed how perpetrators activate the brain's "attachment circuitry" to confuse victims. Once this circuitry is active, the perpetrator can begin to push the victim's boundaries just as George did when he walked down the hall with me and tried to kiss me before becoming aggressive. Moreover, once trust is established, our defense mechanisms are delayed. A victim may not realize until it's too late that she is in danger. She may not be able to process what is happening, such as the consensual sex that turns into a violent rape, or the friendly conversation that slowly turns into a threat or coercion. These confusing situations can cause dissociation where the victim shuts down, not accepting that they are in danger. In mass shootings, for example, witnesses often dissociate.

[vi] The Neurobiology of trauma and interviewing victims.pdf

"What you see in a victim may not be strength or peace. It may be shock."

Laurie Works, a survivor of the mass shooting at New Life Church in Colorado Springs in 2007, saw her twin and younger sisters shot and killed and her father injured. In an essay she wrote for *The Huffington Post*[vii] she described the disconnect between her emotions and her affect, i.e., her expression of these emotions: "What you see in a victim may not be strength or peace. It may be shock. My recounting of the story immediately afterward looked like strength because I didn't break down and cry. In truth, it was not strength or peace; it was shock." She further concluded that it's important not to re-traumatize or re-victimize victims of trauma, noting, "Realize the victims are probably still processing in some way, shape, or form even years later."

It isn't only a mass shooting or other sensational act of violence that causes a victim to live in a state of shock or dissociation. Any trauma can cause this, especially where the trauma is inflicted by someone they trusted. Shock or dissociation may be powerful but not necessarily visible.

Larry Nassar established trust with his victims before assaulting them. Bill Cosby played the role of "America's Dad" so well that few women felt in danger when he invited them to

---

[vii] Supporting Victims in the Aftermath of Mass Shootings | HuffPost Life

his hotel or home. Christopher Duntsch was so assuring to his patients that many agreed to surgeries they didn't even need, including his best friend whom he deliberately left paralyzed. Predators count on establishing trust with their victims to easily lure their prey into situations they might otherwise have avoided.

Kathy McKee said of Bill Cosby, "Bill had been a friend. I had had dinner with his wife on one or two occasions. I had worked with him, I had known him for many, many years, and he never made a pass at me . . . So, when this happened to me, I was really, really shocked. I just couldn't understand what was wrong with him. Had he lost his mind? When I came out of the bathroom, he said to me, 'Okay, come on, let's go. They're waiting for us.' He was behaving like a person I had never met before in my life."[viii] McKee alleges that despite feeling safe and comfortable around Cosby over the years, he attacked her in a hotel room in Detroit one night in 1974 after asking her to bring him some barbecued ribs from a local restaurant. When she brought the ribs to his room he threw them on the floor, pulled up her skirt, and violently raped her. Yet it would take forty years and the reports of many more women before she felt safe enough to tell her story publicly. Throughout those decades, she had internalized the shame feeling that no one would believe her. She was so shocked and confused by her former friend and colleague's behavior that she herself didn't know what to believe.

[viii] 35 Bill Cosby Accusers Tell Their Stories -- The Cut

> *"By the time many do come forward they may even make excuses for the predator, downplaying the victimization and emphasizing their mistakes."*

By the time many do come forward they may even make excuses for the predator, downplaying the victimization and emphasizing their mistakes. When this happens, it's easy to presume they haven't been victimized after all. Like Kathy McKee, many of Bill Cosby's victims thought they were the only ones. They had willingly gone to his home or hotel room, so they felt they had played a role in their own abuse.

Such self-blame is not unfounded. Others can and will blame them for their vulnerability. When legendary record producer Phil Spector shot and killed actress Lana Clarkson in 2003 after she agreed to have a late-night drink with him in his mansion, his first trial ended in a mistrial. In Showtime's documentary series, *Spector,* one juror recalled that another juror remained unwilling to convict despite overwhelming evidence of his guilt because she wondered why Clarkson went home with him in the first place. It's astounding that someone would equate going inside someone's home late at night with consent to being killed, but the tendency to blame the victim—and for victims to blame themselves—is common.

This is why perpetrators often ask their victims to give consent for small acts such as coming home with them—so they can exempt themselves from blame. Ariel Castro in Cleveland had kidnapped, imprisoned, tortured, and repeatedly raped three women in his home for a decade before they finally escaped. During his sentencing, Castro said of one of his victims, "She got into the car without even knowing who I was." In Castro's mind, his victim was to blame for his abuse.

"By assuming that someone played a role in their own victimization . . . you potentially jump to a false and costly conclusion."

So how does victim-blaming play out in an organizational setting?

She had consensual sex with him, so he couldn't have assaulted her. She had drinks with him. She went to his hotel room. She should have known he could be dangerous. She didn't tell him "no" directly. She didn't fight back. She admitted she should have fought harder. She admitted she shouldn't have gone to his hotel room at the conference. She admitted she drank too much. She admitted she'd heard the rumors about his behavior.

By assuming that someone played a role in their own victimization because they either show shame or else failed to act "appropriately"; because they admit to their own mistakes; or because they self-blame, you potentially jump to a false and costly conclusion. These reactions may be stemming from trauma and do not prove they weren't victimized. Be wary of dismissing a report because it bears a whiff of self-blame or victim blaming. Abuse is not just physical. In an organizational setting it almost always involves some form of psychological manipulation intended to confuse the victim and shift the responsibility from the perpetrator to the victim in whole or in part. Don't be manipulated by prior assumptions of how anyone "should" respond to abuse.

How might that confusion, shock, or dissociation appear when someone comes to you or is interviewed concerning a traumatizing experience? The trauma response can take many forms, including:

- **Numbness**—Appearing void of emotion.
- **Inattentiveness**—Not paying attention to what they are being asked or what is said.
- **Substance abuse**—Drinking and drug use are common among survivors of trauma and if someone knows they are going to be questioned about the traumatic event, they may drink or self-medicate with drugs before the interview and appear to lack credibility.
- **Babbling**—Rambling seemingly incoherent and confusing statements; changing the subject.
- **Anger**—Becoming easily triggered by the questioning and lashing out at the interviewers.

Each of these responses can be interpreted as evidence of mental instability, deception, or that the claimant suffered no lasting harm; or these same responses can be evidence of significant harm. Just because you can use such evidence against a claimant doesn't mean it is in your best interest to do so. The more you exacerbate trauma, the more likely a traumatized claimant will pursue justice, ultimately costing you far more both in dollars and reputation.

"The more you exacerbate trauma, the more likely a traumatized claimant will pursue justice, ultimately costing you far more both in dollars and reputation."

WATCH OUT: THESE BIASES CAN SHAPE PERCEPTION

Several other factors influence our perceptions. These factors may have little to do with the facts and everything to do with subjective experience and viewpoints. Beyond the initial emotional response, we are also influenced by:

- Gossip or what others tell about the people involved.
- How much power the involved parties hold in the organization.
- The gender, sexuality, race, age, nationality, religion, or other identities of the parties.
- The manner in which details were revealed.

THE GOSSIP FACTOR

In 2008, a young woman in Lynnwood, Washington, reported a brutal rape. She alleged she had been awoken in the night by an intruder who raped and photographed her. After she was interviewed by police and submitted to a rape exam at a hospital, one of the women's former foster mothers came forward and told police this formerly troubled teen tended to engage in attention-seeking behavior. Hearing that revelation, the police stopped investigating the rape and accused the woman of lying. They then criminally charged her with making a false report, which carried a $500 fine. Soon rumors swirled about the "false allegation," and she was shunned by her friends and the former foster family she had trusted. The rapist went on to attack many more women. It was only after a photo of the bound and naked Lynnwood woman was found in the rapist's possession that her $500 was returned. She then sued the police department, whose reputation was nationally tarnished as a result. On the bright side, the department adopted new training methods for sexual assault investigations and, though it could have been much worse and she could have potentially won a lot more money in court, she decided in the end to settle for a public apology and $150,000.

This case exemplifies many reports of sexual assault. It wasn't the facts of the case that led police to doubt her report, but what they were told *about* the victim. It's natural that police officers would doubt the claim after hearing that the witness shouldn't be believed, especially because there wasn't much evidence of a break in, but if there's one thing my many years of legal practice have taught me, it's that there are no perfect victims. This is especially true in sexual assault and sexual harassment cases where predators often seek out the most emotionally or socially vulnerable targets—those with limited support or with histories of causing problems. They also target the peacemakers—people who would rather avoid trouble or confrontation. These are more likely to try and brush it off. This latter response is often used to undermine claims of unwanted touching or comments, suggesting the victim didn't protest loudly or forcefully enough at the time of the offense.

> *"Even if the person is often unreliable,*
> *that doesn't mean they're making up*
> *the allegation."*

I'm not suggesting you dismiss reports concerning a person's credibility. You should pay attention to such claims but remember: those claims could be gossip and entirely untrue. Even if the person is often unreliable, that doesn't mean they're making up the allegation. The incident may well have happened. Sex workers can be raped; liars can be injured; sick and injured patients can become further sickened or injured by their medical care; and poor-performing workers can be grievously injured on the job through no fault of their own.

What's more, gossip goes both ways. The accused may also be the subject of gossip especially as the investigation unfolds. When the accusations against Larry Nassar first became public, gossip circulated that he was such an amazing doctor and person that he could never have done the things that had been reported. The police were even persuaded by his explanations about the legitimacy of the "medical procedures" he performed on these "rising stars" who needed his expertise and friendship to survive in the tough world of gymnastics where coaches could be cruel and abusive. He was their protector, a friend and supporter of these young women who must have been confused. Similarly, there had been half a dozen reports of Bill Cosby's sexual assaults before they were taken seriously. Cosby's reputation as a model father led investigators to doubt he could be a rapist. Cosby was far too moral. His accusers had to be lying, out to get his money. As a result of his perceived credibility and based on his public image, it was years before a serious investigation was conducted.

> *"As a result of his perceived credibility and based on his public image, it was years before a serious investigation was conducted."*

Gossip can have great impact on organizations. Whenever a report is made of wrongdoing, gossip is going to fly as people try to make sense of which "side" they feel they should take. This gossip is influenced by those in positions of power who may directly or indirectly convey how they hope others will align. Gossip about someone's sexual behavior or sexuality, their mental stability, ethics, or who they are as a person is often spread to deliberately discredit anyone who brings a claim of wrongdoing. Such gossip is often encouraged by management because it can help defeat the claim. It can also make the atmosphere so unpleasant that the claimant becomes angry, confused, anguished, or otherwise limited in their ability to pursue the claim. In my own case, the confusing and invasive nature of the inquiry coupled with the awareness that I might find myself a target of gossip left me so angry and frustrated that I was distracted and had difficulty sleeping. It was hard to open up and get to know others. This all made my already challenging classes more difficult and caused me to isolate.

These experiences are common to claimants who have been traumatized. While many organizations encourage such a commotion to surround those who report wrongdoing—hoping to be rid of the claimant and thus, the problem—healthy organizational cultures avoid and should remain above such retaliatory actions.

THE FOOLISHNESS OF RETALIATION

We all know that it's wrong to retaliate against someone reporting illegal or unethical behavior, but we also know that in some places and due to ignorance retaliation is routine. Retaliation increases the likelihood of litigation, higher damage awards, and greater problems when retaliatory abuse provokes a claimant to aggressive action. Retaliatory acts can sometimes be hard to hide. When members of an organization watch a claimant experience backlash for speaking up, distrust, fear, and secrecy will abound. Secrecy breeds rumors, gossip, and further distrust. Rumors and gossip cause instability. People may turn against each other. They may lose trust in their colleagues and management to the point where they leave the organization. In this kind of toxic environment, stress levels skyrocket while productivity declines. If you want your organization to get through the investigation unscathed and maintain its strong organizational culture, instruct all levels of management and all investigators to:

- Quash rumors and gossip.
- Avoid and discourage retaliation.
- Be as transparent as possible.
- Constantly communicate the grave consequences of libel and retaliatory actions.

As we said earlier, this goes both ways to protect both the

claimant and the accused. Conversely, the organizational culture is undermined by:

- Suggesting guilt before an investigation is complete.
- Blindsiding your witnesses with surprise interviews and interrogations.
- Communicating that the claimant is a problem.

These actions expose you to:

- A less or ineffective investigation.
- Higher risk of litigation.
- Higher damages.
- A hit to your reputation.

Once you've violated these principles and parties become reactive it can be nearly impossible to control the spill. The complaining and disenchantment will not be held in by the walls of your organization but will make their way to the eyes and ears of the public. With social media and the explosion of independent news sources online, this last consequence can result in the greatest long-term, and possibly irrecoverable, damage.

WHEN POWER COMES INTO PLAY

Perhaps the most determinative factor in any internal investigation of wrongdoing is the power of the parties involved. Imagine someone claims that your boss did something egregious. Even if you believe them, you know you'll have to tread carefully because there's only one outcome your boss is going to want—his or her exoneration.

Whether it's your boss, a friend, a superior in another department, or just someone who has formal or informal influence in the organization, as you well know, power aligns with power. Investigative findings are far more likely to be based on who than what.

"Be aware of the pressure you're under as your investigation may be quite politicized, and you may also be subconsciously influenced by people in power."

Who is accused and who claims injury?

Naturally, going after anyone in a position of influence can put those investigating and ruling on the matter on high alert. That's why Harvey Weinstein and Bill Cosby got away with sexual assaults for as long as they did despite claims from several women. No one wanted to cross such influential men.

"I told my supervisor at the Playboy Club," P.J. Masten, one of Cosby's accusers said, "and you know what she said to me? 'You do know that's Hefner's best friend, right?' I said, 'Yes.' She says, 'Nobody's going to believe you. I suggest you shut your mouth.'"[ix]

While you're not likely to be dealing with Hollywood royalty in your investigations, you may end up having to investigate someone with power and influence. So, what are you going to do?

The important thing is to do your job. Investigate in all fairness to all parties. Be aware of the pressure you're under as your

---

[ix] 35 Bill Cosby Accusers Tell Their Stories -- The Cut

investigation may be quite politicized, and you may also be subconsciously influenced by people in power. It is human nature to avoid danger. Investigating someone with potential influence over your own job is dangerous. Consequently, you might unconsciously look for reasons to doubt the credibility of the claimant, dismiss evidence in their favor, or give greater weight to evidence that casts doubt on their claim. Remain alert to your predispositions and keep yourself in the clear by constantly returning to the facts to shape your perception.

"Remain aware of the implicit bias you may experience in an investigation of someone powerful or influential . . . "

If you don't, this subconscious bias is likely to lead you to mistreating someone, and then you can expect to find your mess on full display through social media, news press, and maybe even a lawsuit. Remain aware of the implicit bias you may experience in an investigation of someone powerful or influential, and you're more likely to treat the claimant fairly and humanely, fending off any potential lawsuit or damage to your institution's reputation.

THE BIAS OF RACE AND SOCIAL IDENTITIES

As I write these pages, a ten-year-old black boy has been charged with misdemeanor battery for what's described by him and his family as a harmless hug of his school counselor. The white counselor alleges that the boy put one arm around her shoulder and grabbed her breast with his other hand. The incident happened in full view of the boy's classroom and though the school allegedly declined to investigate the incident, the counselor reported it to the police. Now the counselor has been branded a racist and the boy a sexual deviant. He's been charged with a crime, suspended, and possibly expelled from school.

I don't know the facts of this case. I have no idea if the hug was indeed harmless and misunderstood; whether there was intentional or accidental touching of the counselor's breast; or what actions the school administrators took or failed to take before contacting the police.

All I know is that the incident has already smeared the reputations of the school, the police, the counselor, and a young boy, and that the races of the boy and the counselor—which may or may not have anything to do with the incident or how it was perceived—are now the number one issue in the press.

That is because we live in a society with a long history of racial injustice where, just a few generations ago, black men were routinely lynched anytime someone said they acted inappropriately toward a white woman. Nothing was investigated and people of color were believed to be guilty upon accusation alone. As racial tensions have intensified in recent years with recorded videos of black men and women being assaulted and killed by police, all it takes for an internal claim to become a viral media event is for one party to be of one race and the other of another race.

"The thoughts crossing your mind may reflect your own implicit biases."

If the reported incident involves parties of more than one race, be aware of not only how these racial differences might influence the manner of reporting, but also how your own biases might play a role.

Let's take this case of the boy and the school counselor. The boy and his family allege nothing happened and he is the victim of racist perceptions. The woman alleges the school failed to investigate and address the matter and that she is a victim of sexual assault. What do you think happened?

The thoughts crossing your mind may reflect your own implicit biases. Whether you concluded that it probably did or did not happen, the truth is, if all you've read of the case is what little I've relayed in these pages, then you don't know any more than I know. The press often fails to commit to fact-finding. The few facts we have might not be true facts at all. If the school made assumptions and so failed to investigate, far from getting rid of the problem they may have provoked the counselor to go to the police and to the press.

Social identities are loaded with personal and political histories and stereotypes. These stereotypes are too easily deployed to create or dismiss a claim. If a mentally disabled man is accused of groping a woman, is he like any sexually aggressive male or does his disability preclude him from culpability? Either view is a stereotype and probably doesn't accurately reflect what happened. Seeing through these stereotypes and our biases, conscious or not, helps focus the investigation on the facts and not our assumptions about those involved.

Gender is another loaded social identity that can influence an investigation. You may feel your organization has no problem with gender because men and women are equally represented, but there may be assumptions about how women are to act that differ from expectations of men. Women can be perceived as bitchy, bullies, or harsh just for being as assertive as a man. Likewise, men can be perceived as aggressive and sexist just for being men. A woman who presents a claim of sexual assault or harassment might be dismissed because of how she is dressed, just as a man who presents the same claim might be dismissed because some presume that men can't be sexually assaulted or harassed. We live in a society with different roles and expectations based on gender. Deviating from expectations can trigger others to discredit or dismiss even legitimate claims.

"Just as trauma can shape how an incident or series of incidents is presented, social differences also shape testimony."

In 2018, a miner in West Virginia filed a lawsuit against his mining company alleging sexual harassment. In his suit, he alleged that because he did not appear sufficiently masculine his coworkers verbally harassed him, punched him in the genitals, and threatened to beat him. He also claimed that one worker exposed his genitals to him, tried to force him to touch them, and threatened to rape him. When he reported the abuse to HR, he was allegedly told he was lucky to have a job. He ultimately quit and filed his lawsuit.

One wonders if the lawsuit and adverse publicity could have been avoided entirely by HR taking him seriously, investigating the matter, and taking appropriate action against those who had engaged in such behaviors. Had a woman made the same report, she may well have been treated just as badly. In this case, a man had reported being victimized, defying stereotypes of who gets harassed and how masculinity should be displayed.

Just as trauma can shape how an incident or series of incidents is presented, social differences also shape testimony. A black man or woman reporting a complaint to a white man or woman may be more guarded in how they present their claim as they try to assess your level of comfort in their presence. That doesn't mean they're being deceitful or withholding important facts. It means that if they've been traumatized, they want to be sure they feel comfortable with you. Similarly, a woman being questioned by a man may not reveal everything about a sexual assault or harassment—just as she might hold back from another woman if she senses that woman is judging her.

The important thing to keep in mind is that we live in a society deeply divided by race and gender. Sexuality is another identity that comes loaded with stereotypes and expectations, as is age, religion, nationality, disability, and many others. A young person may be guarded around an older person, just as an older person may have low confidence in a younger person when discussing a disturbing experience. If an older person is struggling to find the right words, hesitates, or is easily confused, a younger person may assume the claim is without merit. The claimant will often pick up on the hearer's doubtfulness and react with further anxiousness and instability.

Our stereotypes and expectations of how people *should* present or interact can shape how others convey details of a traumatic event. The way an investigator initially perceives a witness can persist throughout the entire investigation. Be aware of your own implicit biases and those of the other parties so you can avoid turning a resolvable issue into a PR nightmare.

WHEN DETAILS OF THE STORY CHANGE

As any investigator knows, when someone's story changes with every retelling, there's reason to be suspicious. When new evidence is presented, a witness who suddenly "remembers" something that alters the story, who adds increasingly shocking details with every retelling, or who seems to have simply forgotten the version or versions they've told before is often lying. However, to complicate matters, a traumatized witness may also add or change details and that doesn't mean they're lying.

"One factor affecting the disclosure of details is that most people are not comfortable. They don't feel safe."

So, how can you tell the difference?

First, understand why this happens. One factor affecting the disclosure of details is that most people are not comfortable. They don't feel safe. They may also feel ashamed or guilty even if whatever happened was through no fault of their own. The rape victim who flirted with her attacker may feel she brought it on by flirting, so she omits that detail or even insists otherwise. The crane operator who prides himself on his safety record may feel he must have made a mistake because he hadn't gotten enough sleep the night before, so he leaves out how tired he was or insists he had plenty of rest. Eventually, as time passes, he may disclose the truth and risk casting doubt on his entire testimony. The mother whose child is born with cerebral palsy may lie about missing a prenatal appointment or having a glass of wine while pregnant because she fears she may have caused the disability. In other words, guilt, shame, and remorse all inhibit how we present the details of an incident, especially when reports involve personal or intimate details.

People will be guarded in their initial report. Do not be surprised by this. It doesn't mean they are lying and it doesn't mean they are attempting to manipulate. They need to feel safe and to know that even if they've made mistakes, which may lead to contributory negligence, it doesn't mean they weren't wronged.

". . . an altered memory is not necessarily a false memory or deceit . . . "

Another way traumatized witnesses change the details of an incident is by remembering new details. Someone who is in a traumatized state may not remember every detail. They may not even see every detail, as Russ Faria failed to do when finding his wife's body. Even though she had been stabbed dozens of times, all he saw was the blood. All he could imagine in that moment of shock was that she must have killed herself. Shock can blind us. Shock can also cause us to block out details that are later restored as the shock subsides. That's because trauma causes the memory-storing hippocampus to shrink, producing gaps in our memory. As time passes and the hippocampus heals, we may experience "flashbacks" when something triggers the memory.

"The challenge is to disentangle the truth from the emotional whirlwinds each party brings to the table."

What I hope to convey is that a traumatic event can and will alter the brain and potentially wreak havoc on recall. Understanding that an altered memory is not necessarily a false memory or deceit can help you treat the reporting witness more gently and compassionately, knowing that there may be details that change or don't add up, but *something* happened to traumatize them.

The challenge for investigators is to uncover what that "something" was. That it isn't immediately clear doesn't mean nothing happened. The person who comes to you with a report of injury or wrongdoing is sharing with you their *experience*. You may be uncertain of the chain of events or specific facts, but by taking their experience seriously you are far more likely to find them cooperative and forthcoming.

"Someone traumatized is in a state of fear and often anger. Their memory is battered."

The road to the whole truth is messy. The only certainty you can count on are competing narratives. Narratives conflict, collide, and rarely coincide as you collect information to determine the facts and avoid further damage to your institution.

Let's consider the memory of the one accused. Getting at the truth is not a matter of figuring out who's telling the truth. The challenge is to disentangle the truth from the emotional whirlwinds each party brings to the table. Someone traumatized is in a state of fear and often anger. Their memory is battered. They may or may not be guarded based on how safe or unsafe they feel with you, and their emotions may seem off kilter leading you to question their credibility. That's just the one making the allegation. What about the person or people they've accused of wrongdoing?

FACT OR FICTION: HOW CAN YOU TELL?

The accused may also be traumatized either by the formal investigation, or the incident, or both. They may feel they did nothing so bad as to merit an inquiry. They may feel ashamed or worried they'll be found out for acts they know are wrong. The first thing you need to do is listen.

Listen to how they present themselves. Investigators often overlook the verbal cues that signal deceit.[x] Although there is no definitive marker of a lie, there are certain verbal cues that, put together, may signal deception. If you note a pattern, you might be dealing with someone attempting to deceive you.

If the accused is working hard to align with you, presenting themselves as helping you to clear the whole thing up, be on guard. Someone who has done nothing is more likely to be confused and worried. They may even be angry, but they aren't likely to view themselves and the investigators as on the same team. Perhaps they share a concern for the organization, but they are more likely to view any questioning about their behavior as inherently antagonistic.

"It's normal for an unjustly accused person to be angry, but rarely do they respond with threats during initial questioning."

Do they make threats? Do they make a big show of their moral superiority or display their institutional power and threaten a lawsuit for being falsely accused? Such responses

[x]   Bogaard G., Meijer EH, Vrij A., Merckelbach H. (2016), Strong, but Wrong: Lay People's and Police Officers' Beliefs about Verbal and Nonverbal Cues to Deception. PLoS ONE 11(6): e0156615. https://doi.org/10.1371/journal.pone.0156615.

may be a red flag. They may be trying to stop the investigation in its tracks. It's normal for an unjustly accused person to be angry, but rarely do they respond with threats during initial questioning.

Do they describe the person making the report as emotionally unbalanced? Listen for counter accusations such as: "They're always making complaints," or "That person is nothing but trouble." People who are innocent are more likely to talk about themselves and their actions than they are to focus their responses on someone else.

Someone who harmed another, and who could also be harmed if found culpable, is not going to want to tell the truth. They'll want the investigation to stop. They'll want to persuade you that they are innocent. They may become overly solicitous or threatening or swing back and forth between the two.

How about the person who is innocent of wrongdoing?

". . . completely shutting people out and refusing to discuss the matter with them due to advice from the legal department will just enrage them."

They, too, will be worried. Over time they may threaten litigation if they feel they are being falsely accused. Still, they aren't likely to attempt to manipulate you, gaslight the one making the report, or point to their moral or institutional superiority. It is likely they will be traumatized. Recognize the signs.

One of the biggest mistakes made in an organizational investigation is prejudgment. When you have conflicting narratives, the best strategy toward getting at the facts is to treat everyone humanely and listen closely. Interrupting, telling them they are wrong, expressing doubt, and cross-examining may work in an interrogation, but in an institutional investigation those tactics will not get to the truth. It will shut people down. Further, completely shutting people out and refusing to discuss the matter with them due to advice from the legal department will just enrage them. Any form of shunning or social punishment will likely exacerbate the sense of injustice and harm.

It's not at all unusual for an organization to present its investigations as fair and objective despite investigators' singular goal —not to uncover the truth but to protect the organization. These investigations become mere veneers of inquiry intended only to steer towards a certain outcome. *USA Today* investigated 107 public universities with universities with fifty-six responding. They found that of the "tens of thousands" of reports of sexual misconduct at these universities over a seven-year period, just 1,094 students were suspended and only 594 students were expelled. Some reading these numbers may interpret this to mean there have been tens of thousands of false reports, but the report concluded: "Confusing policies allowed schools to avoid investigating cases and steer reports toward outcomes that required minimal action."

By minimizing the number of students found culpable for sexual offenses, the universities protected their image above their students. Universities can also control statistics by delaying their findings until the accused students are no longer enrolled, in which case they don't have to complete the investigation. This is what happened with my complaint at Harvard.

PLAY IT SMART

If you or your organization set out to quash complaints brought to your attention and prove that those who bring the complaints lack credibility, you aren't protecting your organization. You're making it vulnerable to greater damage when someone who feels they haven't been treated fairly or humanely goes public with their complaint.

Successful organizational leadership requires processes that work. Educate interviewers and those who take initial reports on how trauma can shape the way facts are presented, why certain facts may initially be withheld, and how implementing a trauma-informed investigative process can protect the organization. Properly handling the situation from the start protects you far more than trying to quash.

"There are unlimited paths you can take to get at the truth, but avoid any path that could be construed as treating the claimant crudely or unfairly."

Look at the bigger picture before you attempt to put all the data into context. There are unlimited paths you can take to get at the truth, but avoid any path that could be construed as treating the claimant crudely or unfairly. In pivotal moments throughout the investigative process, how you serve those who feel unjustly wronged can and will alter the direction the investigation takes and the end you reach.

So, make the very first touchpoint along the way—taking the initial report—one that feels safe and non-confrontational. Don't re-traumatize or dehumanize them. Regardless of what the facts may be, the best way to get to the truth is to help everyone involved feel safe, respected, and treated with compassion. In the next chapter, I'll discuss how a good or bad outcome can be determined from any touchpoint in the process.

CHAPTER 5

REFORMING THE PROCESS

E very organization has at least some process in place for reporting acts of wrongdoing; yet, even before it has been formally initiated, it's likely the person has already taken informal steps. In my case, I took steps to document what had happened. I photographed my bruises, met with George to discuss the incident, and reached out to two of my classmates for advice and support in case of another incident. True, I am an attorney and understand the importance of documentation, but many people will have some sense of why it's important to document their injuries.

Most just need to be heard. People who are hurt typically vent. They may reach out to a friend, a colleague, or someone who works in the institution; their nurse who has been caring for them, a trusted professor, or that secretary who knows just what to do.

Your job isn't to train these random people on trauma, nor can you. The first person someone turns to can be anyone, and whoever that is becomes a witness. That person will also influence the next steps taken in the reporting process. When Ben told me I'd been assaulted, the reality and gravity of George's actions hit me for the first time. I immediately felt validated, yet angrier, because I knew he was right. When I acknowledged the offense was not just rude but unlawful behavior, my need to take action grew. George posed a threat not just to me, but to other women in the program and to the school itself. I felt a moral obligation to alert those in positions of authority.

"Most people making reports of wrongdoing feel they are informing the institution of a problem, not creating that problem."

As I've noted, it's common to perceive the person making the report as the risk or threat to your institution. No one likes a tattletale, and the bearer of bad news is never welcomed. The potential for this person to become a litigant or whistleblower leads many to take immediate defensive action and do whatever they can to quash the matter. The one coming forward, however, usually intends to do just the opposite of putting the institution at risk. Most people making reports of wrongdoing feel they are informing the institution of a problem, not creating that problem. When you treat the person coming forward not as putting you at risk but *alerting* you to risk, you ease their anxiety and begin the process on a cooperative note. Viewing them as complainers will ignite an adversarial process, which escalates the threat of litigation. To avoid an adversarial process, recognize the varying touchpoints along the way and how these touchpoints can become turning points—either escalating the conflict or resolving the matter as constructively and early as possible.

ESTABLISH A CLEAR CHANNEL OF COMMUNICATION

I had noticed the sign on the women's restroom door enough times that when I decided to report George, I knew exactly where to find the number. Making that initial call was hard. I was concerned I would set into motion a bureaucratic and legal machinery that might publicize my disturbing encounter with George. I'd survived childhood sexual abuse and told almost no one about it. I instinctively safeguard my privacy, but I also feared George's aggression would intensify, and my need for privacy became secondary to my sense of responsibility. I had to take action. I was responsible for my own safety, and I felt morally obligated to alert my classmates and the school that a sexual aggressor was among us.

So, I built up the courage to make that call only to be told they couldn't speak to me! Imagine my sense of defeat when I was told this "emergency" number was for other kinds of students.

I felt deflated. I felt diminished, as if I didn't matter as much as the students in the MBA program. At a time when I needed help, instead I felt excluded. What's more, I wasn't given another number to call. Finding out who to call was up to me. There was no clear channel of communication. My confusion and anger mounted.

"Remember that the person making a report is often in a state of confusion. They can't make clear decisions. Make it easy for them to understand the steps."

Every organization needs a clear channel of communication for reporting wrongdoing. If you're going to use a hotline, designate one specifically for raising a grievance of wrongdoing. Whether it's a hotline, an HR officer, a form to complete, or whatever initial contact method you've established for reporting a grievance. Keep that information clearly posted and be sure the process is simple and straightforward. Remember that the person making a report is often in a state of confusion. They can't make clear decisions. Make it easy for them to understand the steps. This is the first touchpoint in a reporting process designed to *mitigate* damage. If you offer a bewildering array of phone numbers for different types of people to report different types of complaints, you will establish a turning point that causes confusion, frustration, or even anger in an already shaken or traumatized person.

Have a central number for anyone to call. If different classes of people such as students, staff, clients, or guests need to speak with different departments, make sure whoever answers that central number can transfer the caller to the appropriate hotline. Publish the entire phone list with clear labeling so that administrators know which phone number they should call. If it is not possible to have a twenty-four-hour hotline, be sure the hours of operation are noted. No one should have to look around for the right number or call the number posted only to be told they need to research another number. They're traumatized, scared, worried and confused. Don't make it worse. Post the numbers in a single publication and don't hide this publication. Make the information easy to find on your website. Put it clearly and plainly in handbooks you distribute. Post fliers visibly in every department and in high traffic areas such as the dorms, cafeteria, common lounge, and other places where people will likely see it. If call hours are limited, provide a message indicating where a person should call in an emergency, even if that is offsite such as a local community sexual assault hotline.

How that initial call or in-person visit is handled will shape what follows. No one coming forward with their concerns wants to be treated as a troublemaker, much less a liar or mentally unstable. Often, a new complainant does not want to engage in a formal investigation. They want to alert someone in case the problem worsens. Maybe they want advice or to put the institution on notice that a problem might ensue, but they prefer to keep it low key and quietly move on with their life. They may well appear mentally unstable due to their trauma, but they deserve to be treated as people both asking for help and also warning the institution of a potential problem.

Once a person has made an initial report, they'll want to know the next steps. This is where you may create differing processes depending on the concern raised and the size of your institution. There may be one process for reporting sexual assault or harassment and another for medical malpractice or personal injury. What's important is that this process is clear and understandable. Setting clear expectations for "what happens next" empowers the person coming forward and gives them some sense of control over what follows in the process. Without that clarity, the claimant may never feel confident they've taken the right steps to do the right thing and may fear they've just been spinning their wheels. This makes an already unnerving experience with your institution even worse.

"A traumatized person needs choices so they can be in the driver's seat of their role in the process."

Nevertheless, the nature of the problem, such as sexual assault of a minor, might necessitate an investigation regardless of the desires of the complainant. If at some point during reporting the institution is compelled by law to open a formal inquiry within or outside the organization, inform the complainant and be sure they understand the inquiry is mandatory due to the nature of the complaint.

From there, things can rapidly get out of control with gossip, publicity, and organizational chaos as we've discussed. Before you know it, that first touchpoint has become a turning point that upends careers, breeds gossip that threatens relationships and takes the matter into the public arena where reputations are destroyed. You don't want that and the person coming forward probably doesn't either. Thus, be sure anyone coming forward understands what is likely to happen once the report is officially submitted. Explain the process and how much control they will be able to exercise over it. A traumatized person needs choices so they can be in the driver's seat of their role in the process. If they feel they have lost control over what happens next, they may become desperate to reign in the process. The more they understand their options and how the process works, the better. Provide that clarity from the start and at every step, and <u>make sure the people fielding calls are properly trained to provide trauma-informed responses.</u>

ADMINISTRATORS

Very often the first place a person will formally report a problem is with the head of a department or program, though other administrators or risk managers may be the initial contact. When the hotline number got me nowhere, I took the next logical step and went to the program director. This is usually a first touchpoint and it's the one most likely to be fraught with political landmines. The head of any department or program usually knows at least one of the parties involved, if not from experience, from reputation or status.

"If the complainant wants something done and nothing happens, this touchpoint is likely to become a turning point for the worse . . . "

Regardless of "zero tolerance" policies or personal intentions, the reality is that the first thing a department or program head is likely to consider is the political fallout. That's how organizations operate. The social networks established in the organization are key to professional success. Consequently, it's important that these administrators feel safe to initiate an inquiry if necessary. It's equally important that they take action if the person making the report wants something done. As I've said, if the administrator is legally compelled to initiate a formal investigation, then that is what they must do regardless of the complainant's intent.

That is not often the case.

Most often, the complainant and administrator can determine whether any action is taken. If the complainant wants something done and nothing happens, this touchpoint is likely to become a turning point for the worse as the person wronged pursues action by contacting administrators at higher levels, going to the press, and/or filing a lawsuit. To prevent or limit such actions, there are several steps a department or program head can take.

First, offer the complainant the option of joining the initial conversation or deferring, and then have a conversation with the accused and others involved. Often, key facts are initially unknown as in a medical malpractice claim or an on-the-job catastrophic injury. In many cases, a simple conversation will be sufficient to clarify the problem. In these cases, because memory fades and changes rapidly, it's important to interview the primary witnesses as soon as possible.

As you know, not everyone is truthful, particularly when careers and reputations are on the line. In many cases, the person or people accused may deny that anything happened. The department or program head is then left having to weigh the credibility of all parties. That's where mistakes can happen. We tend to think we're good at spotting liars, but most of us are no better than fifty-fifty. Even trained police officers only spot liars around 56 percent of the time, which is not much more than by chance.[i] Everyone was convinced Larry Nassar was a stellar

---

i   Frontiers | Accuracy, Confidence, and Experiential Criteria for Lie Detection Through a Videotaped Interview (frontiersin.org).

physician. Bill Cosby was the charming and funny actor with high moral character. When we throw subjective perceptions into the mix we are much more likely to inaccurately gauge the credibility of two competing stories.

". . . rather than focus on the consequences of initiating an investigation, the administrator should focus on the consequences of not taking action."

For this reason, administrators on the frontlines of the reporting process must keep in mind the possibility—or probability—that the report is true. I'm not suggesting that anyone be judged guilty at this point. I'm suggesting that all reports be taken seriously. I'm also suggesting that rather than focus on the consequences of initiating an investigation, the administrator should focus on the consequences of *not* taking action.

When Joe Paterno was head coach at Penn State and a teaching assistant told him he had witnessed Jerry Sandusky raping a young boy in the shower, Paterno's focus was on the fallout of the investigation. Rather than report the matter to the police as required by law, he reported a watered-down version of events to the athletic director and the vice president of finance and business, where the matter was quickly hushed. As a consequence, many more boys were raped and molested before Assistant Coach Sandusky was caught and convicted. Paterno was fired in disgrace and died within a few months. His concern for the consequence of the investigation led to far greater consequences for the university, the children, and their families, and ultimately his own life.

MY HANDS-ON EDUCATION

The program director connected me with their human resources (HR) director, who then informed me she was going to bring my report to the Office of General Council (OGC) and the Office of Gender Equity (OGE). I assumed I'd get to talk with them myself, but that didn't happen. Instead, my HR contact spoke privately with these two offices and then let me know she was going to interview George.

That seemed reasonable enough, but my stomach was churning. *What would he say? What would they think? What would they do?* I could barely study, barely focus on my classes. I'd taken a drastic step and there was no going back. *Did I do the right thing?* They seemed to believe me. Surely I'd done the right thing. They needed to know about a guy like him in their program, not just for my protection, but for the protection of other students and the program's reputation. *Of course they'll do something . . . but then what will George do?*

I didn't have to wait long. Within a few hours she called to inform me that she'd met with George and other university representatives and they'd made a decision. I took a deep breath. *Good, they're doing something. I'll be safe.*

George and I would both be issued a no-contact order.

As an attorney I understood the mutual no-contact order but issuing me a no-contact order felt like a slap in the face. She continued to explain that George would be removed from my living group and classes and they'd move him to another room in the same hall . . .

. . . but he wouldn't be removed from the program.

"Now that I'd reported him, I felt even more unsafe."

Under Title IX, even if they determined that he had violated the Harvard Business School's Code of Conduct, George was entitled to the protections of a Title IX investigation before he could be kicked out. If I chose *not* to file a formal Title IX complaint, there was no action they were permitted to take under the law. I knew if I chose to file a complaint, the investigative process would take far longer than the remaining weeks left in the program.

In other words, the very law intended to protect victims can be used against them.

I was stunned. Title IX was supposed to protect *me*. As an attorney, I understand the rights of the accused in a court of law, but this was not a court of law. This was an institution with its own right to establish standards of conduct. The institution has the right to evaluate and judge to protect its reputation and the people they serve. Wasn't that the whole reason we signed agreements promising to abide by "Community Values and Guidelines"?

"But what about your 'Community Values'?" I asked her. "Don't those mean anything?"

In reply, she explained that Title IX superseded their own guidelines. Because the matter was sexual in nature, it had to conform to the provisions of Title IX.

I didn't understand. Perhaps as an attorney I did, but after what had happened to me, I developed a new understanding of what it meant to be assaulted by someone in my daily environment. I was genuinely frightened of this man. I didn't feel safe in their program because of his actions. Now that I'd reported him, I felt even more unsafe.

"So, he's denying it?" I asked, thinking about his presumption of innocence and right to bring evidence against me.

No, he wasn't denying it. In some cases, the initial conversation doesn't produce a denial but a partial admission. He admitted that the encounter happened as I'd described it, though he said he didn't recall holding me hard enough to cause any bruises. He assured her he'd apologized. That, in his view, apparently settled the matter.

After some soothing assurances, she added that he had a right to complete the program but for safety reasons, he would not be permitted to join any other living group.

"If he isn't considered safe enough to be in a living group, how is he safe enough to be in the program? And how is moving him to another room in the same building where I live supposed to provide me with any safety or comfort? I'm afraid to leave my room. I'm afraid to walk down the hall to get a cup of coffee because he could be waiting for me. I don't feel safe knowing he's here."

I felt my heart rate accelerate and my ears burn as the blood rushed to my head. I'd thought that by coming forward I was putting an end to my fear. Instead, it seemed I'd just given George cause to be even angrier with me. Now he might view himself as the victim, and I was still going to have to face him.

"What supportive measures would you like us to provide?" she asked me.

I wanted to trust her. I wanted to empathize with her, view her as a woman who wanted to help but was powerless to do so given the implications of Title IX, but I already didn't trust her.

Justly or not, I saw her as doing more to protect George than to protect me.

"I want you to enforce the Community Value Guidelines of Harvard Business School," I told her. "His behavior was a violation of those guidelines, and he should be removed for violating them."

When I met with her and the program director initially, they both assured me those guidelines were meaningful, and that people could be removed for a lot less. I wondered if there were students who'd been kicked out for smoking pot in their room or just for their drunken behavior, behavior that didn't involve sexual misconduct. Ironically, because George's behavior had involved a sexual assault, he seemed more protected than had he just stumbled around drunkenly and knocked a marble bust off its pedestal.

"Somehow, by coming forward and doing what I thought was the right and smart thing to do . . . , all I'd managed to do was make myself more vulnerable."

The program director and faculty co-chairs agreed that George's behavior met the standard for removal from the program, but they couldn't take any action. In other words, their "Community Values and Guidelines" were meaningless if the violation was an assault that was sexual in nature. Later, one of my professors posed the hypothetical, "So, if he had punched her in the face we could kick him out, but because it was sexual in nature there's nothing we can do?" Sadly, he was correct.

"I wish I could do more," the HR liaison said, "but my hands are tied." Then she thanked me for bringing the matter to her attention and added the obligatory, "If you have any more problems with him . . ." and "rest assured" and "we have on-campus mental health support" and "thank you" and "goodbye."

I hung up the phone in shock. Somehow, by coming forward and doing what I thought was the right and smart thing to do to protect myself, other women, and everyone involved, all I'd managed to do was make myself more vulnerable.

The foremost concern of any institution needs to be protecting those entrusted to its care. If anyone violates its standards or puts others at risk, they must be removed from the group. By erring to the side of caution and taking meaningful action to protect others, including the complainant, your institution is less likely to suffer damage to its reputation or face unnecessary claims for damages.

Upon hearing a grievance, most administrators or managers will immediately inform someone else, just as the program director went straight to HR and a few others. Her reasoning was sound—she wanted to take appropriate action. Once she did, five people from the institution were not only aware of the problem but they also became involved. Each of these five then contributed their opinion to the final decision. This has pros and cons.

Almost always, someone will suggest shutting the matter down.

As I've previously indicated, there will be someone who disparages the person bringing the complaint, branding them as a liar, too sensitive, making too much out of nothing, trying to make a buck—whatever it takes to dissuade people from taking the matter seriously. There is often talk about scandal and the need to make the problem go away by pretending it didn't happen. As these multiple management-level players discuss the matter, they form a consensus. That consensus can easily shift the focus from the facts to the strategic steps needed to achieve their agreed-upon goal, such as making the problem go away.

"The more the people on the frontlines attempt to make the problem go away by denying it or discrediting the one raising the issue, the more likely the problem will get bigger . . . "

The more the people on the frontlines attempt to make the problem go away by denying it or discrediting the one raising the issue, the more likely the problem will get bigger as rumors and gossip can reshape memory and history. We've already discussed gossip and how it can influence perception. Now let's take a closer look at rumors and how you can control them before they end up controlling your investigation.

CONTROLLING RUMORS

We tend to think of rumors and gossip as the same thing, but they are two distinct phenomena. In their book, *Rumor Psychology: Social and Organizational Approaches,* psychologists Nicholas DiFonzo and Prashant Bordia note that rumors involve the communication of discrete pieces of information that are often, though not always, true. Rumors are generated to make sense of an ambiguous situation or to help people adapt to perceived threats. Unfortunately, rumors can quickly become distorted and exaggerated over time, particularly when there is limited information about what is really happening.

Once interviews are underway, the proverbial cat is out of the bag. When management questions witnesses about someone's sexual behaviors but refuses to disclose the nature of the investigation, the hush-hush atmosphere is likely to provoke rumors of sexual harassment that can quickly turn to rumors of sexual assault—even if no sexual assault was involved. Transparency limits the likelihood of rumors growing more extreme and outlandish as the plain truth eliminates the need for conjecture.

"After not quashing the rumors, the university subjected . . . themselves to a lawsuit that cost them several hundred thousand dollars . . . and also plummeted them into a morass of internal investigations and external bad press."

In her book, *Mobbed! What to Do When They Really Are Out to Get You,*[ii] anthropologist Janice Harper wrote of how rumors spun wildly out of control when she applied for tenure at her university. After she reported behavior that could be construed as sexual harassment, her department head said she "lacked collegiality" for not having resolved the conflict privately and should therefore be denied tenure.

---

ii   Harper, Janice (2016), *Mobbed! What to Do When They Really Are Out to Get You,* Seattle: Backdoor Press.

As management initiated interviews with her colleagues about the alleged sexual harassment, the rumors that she "lacked collegiality" soon shifted to "she's lying" to "she's crazy" to "she's making threats of killing herself" to "she's making threats of killing others" to "she's building a hydrogen bomb." One student remarked that though she had never known Harper to be violent or say anything about violence, she had heard so many rumors that she concluded that Harper's class lecture on the atomic bomb was actually a coded threat to build one!

After not quashing the rumors, the university subjected Harper to a Homeland Security investigation that fully exonerated her. They subjected themselves to a lawsuit that cost them several hundred thousand dollars, could have cost them more had it gone to trial, and also plummeted them into a morass of internal investigations and external bad press.

As Harper's case demonstrates, rumors that aren't addressed and quashed immediately can become increasingly hyperbolic over time. Harper was conducting research on nuclear weapons, which made her vulnerable to related accusations. Rarely will rumors reach such extremes as being accused of building a hydrogen bomb, but they often become damaging and libelous to both the institution and the people involved. When that happens, an atmosphere of fear and mistrust emerges. This can have far-reaching consequences for the organization. Hearing the rumors, Harper's student became fearful that her professor's lectures were coded threats to bomb a building.

Rumors surrounding an internal investigation more commonly focus on claims that someone is guilty of negligence, malfeasance, theft, or other criminal activity. While rumors typically target those with minimal power in the organization, they can rapidly escalate up the chain of command until rumors of serious wrongdoing at the top organizational levels come to be viewed as fact. If this happens, people may leave. If word gets out, stock prices can fall. Darkness is fertile ground for such rumors to grow and the more that false rumors are not addressed, the more likely they'll be taken as truth.

"Most importantly: address rumors early on."

That said, rumors can lead to useful information when they attract substantiating information as people begin acknowledging their own experiences. Rumors can lead to new witnesses and even victims coming forth. These witnesses can become invaluable aids to any investigation, but management must immediately determine whether the rumor is from a true witness presenting credible evidence, or someone jockeying for attention and information. To make that determination, clarify the nature of the investigation to bring a stop to the social conjecturing and whispering, and interview those spreading rumors. Most importantly: address rumors early on.

How do you do that?

- <u>Do not create a climate that encourages the spread of rumors.</u> At the first whiff of a rumor, meet with those who are spreading it. Inquire as to the evidence supporting the rumor and make it clear that the organization is no place for an inquisition. Inform the

person reporting the rumor that they are not to
spread it.

- <u>Firmly inform the person spreading the rumors of the
  damage they risk</u> to themselves and the organization
  should they continue.
- <u>If a rumor may have merit, contact the investigators</u>
  and request that they interview the person making the
  report along with anyone else involved in spreading
  the rumor.
- <u>Advise the individual(s) to cease from speaking about
  the rumor.</u> Rumors are potentially defamatory and
  can expose your organization to a lawsuit.

WORKING TOWARD AN EFFECTIVE RESOLUTION

---

*". . . the best way to minimize the potential of
an unhappy person filing a lawsuit, contacting
reporters, or venting on social media is to
listen to them wholeheartedly."*

People bring problems to the attention of management to
alert them to a problem and/or because they want help. Treating
these people as a threat backfires. I have learned this not only
from my experience as a personal injury attorney, but as president of my law firm. When clients are unhappy with their
attorney they come to me. In my experience, the best way to
minimize the potential of an unhappy person filing a lawsuit,
contacting reporters, or venting on social media is to listen to

them wholeheartedly. Make sure they know that you care about helping them and fixing the problem in your organization. Show them empathy and honestly assure them that you will investigate the matter.

These early meetings become the second series of touchpoints where the person bringing a grievance senses whether or not they will be taken seriously. In my case, in the initial aftermath of George's attack, I was torn up inside and spent my weekend debating whether I should say anything. Some may mistakenly conclude that my delay meant the incident was not serious. Indeed, I was questioned later about why I'd waited. This felt like a direct blow to me because, from my perspective, I waited because I was taking the matter seriously enough to intentionally weigh the consequences. Their questioning left me feeling they weren't taking my report seriously. What I needed to be told from the onset was that the matter would be investigated. I also needed to be told that, given the sexual nature of the assault, whatever action they ultimately took would have to comply with Title IX. In my case, many of the problems that ensued stemmed from lack of knowledge that Title IX superseded conflicting school policies. Your organization's policies and standards must be consistent with federal and state laws.

If the complainant seeks meaningful action and/or the law mandates further investigation, then the next step is to refer the matter to internal investigation. In cases such as Sandusky's involving the rape of young boys, law enforcement must be notified to conduct their own investigations; but in this book, I focus on the internal investigation. What is it and how does this next touchpoint become constructive rather than a destructive turning point?

ENSURING OBJECTIVE INVESTIGATIONS

In many cases regardless of the law, once someone comes

forward, an investigation is launched. Internal investigations are commonly headed by people untrained or poorly trained in investigative techniques. They typically consider themselves "fact finders," yet these investigators frequently pursue not facts, but a narrative that they feel safeguards the institution's interests despite that a poorly managed investigation can escalate an institution's exposure to litigation. All involved parties may feel defensive, exposed, their privacy violated, and their careers and reputations threatened, making the investigation potentially the most volatile step in the process.

"The first question to ask in any investigation is not toward any of the parties, but toward the institution."

Even expressing faith in the complainant's claim and the likely outcome risks unnecessary anger. In my case, the investigators initially assured me that if George had done what I'd said he'd done, he should be removed from the program. I knew I was telling the truth so that's what I expected would happen. When George admitted to it and was not removed from the program, I felt deceived. Even though the investigators had acted with good intent and genuinely believed they would be able to remove him, they erred in leading me to believe a specific outcome was forthcoming. When that didn't transpire, I was frustrated and confused.

It is critical to the integrity of your investigation that no one be assured of or threatened with any specific outcome until the investigation is complete. The parties may be told a range of possible outcomes, but do not lead anyone to believe that a named outcome is assured.

The investigative process is usually triggered as soon as a report of wrongdoing has been submitted. How do you ensure an objective investigation?

The first question to ask in any investigation is not toward any of the parties, but toward the institution. Who do the investigators report to and are there any potential conflicts of interest?

Harper notes that when she reported an instructor's abusive and sexually harassing behavior, the instructor himself had minimal status at the university but his best friend was the university's interim president who took it upon himself to oversee the investigation. Not surprisingly, the investigators determined without any investigation that the instructor would be treated as the unfortunate victim and the complainant as untruthful. Harper was early informed that if she could not "prove" her allegations, she'd lose her job. Allegations were then distorted by investigators to appear petty and absurd. They never called her witnesses. The questioning turned accusatory. Before long, a veritable witch-hunt ensued in which every email the complainant had ever sent from her university computer was not only reviewed, but selectively circulated to others, mocked, and read aloud to shame her, even though the emails had nothing to do with the allegations. All the while, the investigators reported regularly to the university president, following his direction on how to proceed. This behavior cost the university considerable reputational damage, extensive legal costs, and $300,000 in compensation to Harper.

In an even costlier case, the California Court of Appeals ruled that U.S. Bank National Association owed over $17 million to an employee who was terminated to avoid paying his substantial bonus. Over $15 million of this award was punitive damages. At issue in this settlement was the way the investigation was handled. Administrators accepted evidence against the targeted employee without question while evidence supporting him was dismissed. They ignored conflicts of interest among witnesses and failed to question the motives of witnesses testifying against him. The investigator testified that "the accused gets the opportunity to address accusations on a case-by-case basis. She did not know if [the Plaintiff] had any facts, documents, or witnesses to refute the allegations and did not care if he had any such contradictory evidence."[iii]

"One of the hallmarks of a biased investigation is the refusal to hear witnesses who might substantiate the allegations."

One of the hallmarks of a biased investigation is the refusal to hear witnesses who might substantiate the allegations. Often an allegation is judged based on whether or not others have made complaints. With certain claims, such as sexual harassment or assault, it's often presumed that if a pattern on the part of the accused is lacking, then the isolated allegation is suspect. Indeed, it may be in the best interest of your organization *not* to find any such pattern, but refusing to even look for the pattern increases the risk that your investigation will appear biased. Your complainant is then more likely to seek out someone who

---

[iii] SgB (aboutblaw.com).

will find that pattern, such as an investigative reporter. To be clear, patterns are purposefully ignored by:

- Neglecting to contact witnesses.
- Limiting interviews to people currently associated with your organization while excluding anyone formerly associated with the organization.
- Ignoring previously closed investigations.
- Focusing only on identical allegations rather than other allegations of wrongdoing that might suggest patterns of escalation or of poor judgment.

At the same time, it's not unusual for an internal investigation to appear biased by seeking out negative patterns with the claimant over and above that of the accused. Doing so might land you in the same position as the U.S. Bank National Association, which paid dearly for their biased investigation.

AVOID SECRECY

Problems also emerge when investigations are conducted in secret. Most organizations are advised by legal counsel to keep the investigation as secretive as possible. Counsel hopes that doing so will minimize workplace conflict and prevent comparing and coordinating of testimonies, but taking this advice to the extreme can backfire. Interviewees may be given no explanation other than some vague phrasing about "a matter brought to the attention of management." Even worse, the main parties to the matter are shut out, having no say in who is questioned, what evidence is gathered, or any part of the investigative process. The organization fears a pending lawsuit and so instructs staff not to discuss the matter with anyone, and they may even instruct them not to communicate with the claimant.

I've already spoken about how this silence can infuriate and re-traumatize someone who has already been traumatized, but another thing happens, as well. The witnesses being questioned will start to compare notes. Even if they've been told not to discuss the matter, most will. This is where rumors fly, misinformation spreads, and everyone feels on edge. Rumors and misinformation can easily spread to the internet as anonymous posts are made, often naming the organization and people involved in an effort to condemn someone's alleged behavior.

The risk of facing claims of slander, libel, tortious interference with business relations, or other charges climbs rather than diminishes with a hushed investigation because the very act of calling for silence breeds fear and uncertainty. To prevent the issue from igniting a firestorm of rumors, allegations, and anxiety, be clear about what's going on with the witnesses involved:

- Inform all witnesses concerning the nature of the allegation.
- Remind witnesses that you do not know all the facts, but that once you do, you'll take appropriate action and keep them informed.
- Emphasize the importance of not damaging anyone's reputation or putting anyone at risk during the investigation stage.
- Focus on the nature of the allegations, not the people involved.
- Above all, do not imply that the allegation is with or without merit. Neither assume guilt nor innocence.

It's not uncommon for the accused to be kept in the dark, just as it's not uncommon for the complainant to find themselves completely shut out, causing tensions to rise. When witnesses are questioned without explanation, rumors and tensions will rise. Therefore, anyone who is questioned, accused, or makes an allegation needs to be kept in the loop. What does that loop look like?

- Witnesses and parties are advised not to post anything on social media.
- Witnesses and parties are advised not to take any action that could be construed as retaliation against any party.
- Witnesses and parties are assured that they will be updated when the investigation is complete and findings are made, and protocols are in place to ensure this happens as promised.
- Witnesses and parties are assured that they can present any additional information or evidence at any time.

"While a predetermined outcome can be achieved by any sham investigation, the repercussions are costly."

Unfortunately, many organizations fail to take these steps, and sloppy or biased investigations become breeding grounds for bad press, lawsuits, and organizational chaos. Don't make the same mistakes. While a predetermined outcome can be achieved by any sham investigation, the repercussions are costly. The one being treated unfairly will know they are not being heard and that an unfair investigation is underway. Already traumatized, the institution's unfair or even hostile treatment will provoke the claimant to find justice often by way of litigation, social media, and the press.

To ensure that sham investigations do not put your institution at risk, consider these features of a risky internal investigation:

The risk: The investigation is under the direction or review of someone who is a party to the issue in question, or someone with a personal interest in the outcome.

The remedy: Appoint someone else to direct the investigation and ensure that no one with a conflict of interest and/or undue influence over the outcome can review the investigative procedures. If necessary, appoint an alternative investigative panel or even bring in an outside team of investigators. Never communicate to the investigators the findings you want them to conclude.

The risk: Investigators expressed assurances or beliefs about the outcome early in the investigation.

The remedy: First, be sure your investigators are trained and educated regarding the process and any applicable laws so that they don't mistakenly promise a certain outcome. Any preconceived leanings signal lack of objectivity and may prepare the claimant for a painful disappointment. If an investigator or administrator indicates that they know what the investigation will reveal before commencing, you may need to replace the investigators.

The risk: Investigators expressed political or social beliefs that suggest they will be unable to fairly assess the evidence, witnesses, and parties to the conflict.

The remedy: Train or replace the investigators. You want investigators who are trained in working with a diverse range of witnesses, who will be sensitive to cross-cultural differences in communication styles, and who can work with sensitivity regardless of a person's race, gender, sexuality, nationality, age, or other social identity. These same investigators must be willing and able to set aside their personal biases to legitimately find out what happened and how it happened.

The risk: Investigators have sole discretion over the witnesses they interview and the evidence they gather.

The remedy: Provide the claimant and the accused the opportunity to provide a list of potential witnesses and evidence they believe will support their positions. While it seemingly makes sense for the investigators to have the final decision in who to contact, as U.S. Bank National Association discovered, by refusing to contact the plaintiff's witnesses and review evidence, their investigation was found to be unfair and contributed to the costly verdict against the institution.

The risk: Investigators were appointed internally but have no meaningful training in interviewing techniques, fact finding, identifying witnesses, or identifying and analyzing evidence.

The remedy: Ensure that everyone with an investigatory role is trained in these methods, that this training is ongoing and periodically renewed, and that the training reflects a trauma-informed response. You <u>do not</u> want investigators trained in interrogation methods and who treat witnesses like suspects. You want them trained to listen, to put everyone at ease, and to ask open-ended, follow-up, and probing questions without accusatory tones or statements.

The risk: The investigation is conducted in such secrecy that no one knows what's going on. Too much secrecy is guaranteed to set the rumor mill ablaze producing more false allegations, rupturing relationships, damaging reputations, and reducing productivity as everyone tries to figure out what's going on. The claimant and the accused are likely to become angry, confused, and further traumatized.

The remedy: Keep the main parties informed throughout the process. That does not mean you disclose everything, detail your investigative strategy, or signal you've reached any conclusions. It means you provide timely and consistent updates on the progress, being as specific as you can without disclosing confidential information.

The risk: Evidence is missing or altered. In this high-tech age, it is not uncommon for evidence to be digitally altered, email communications falsified, and important documents destroyed or missing.

The remedy: Safeguard the chain of custody of evidence and document it. Cross-check any printed electronic communication with its source to be sure it was not altered.

By following these guidelines for your investigation process, you are far more likely to ease tensions, calm tempers, minimize gossip, and protect your institution in the event of a legal claim against you. By not merely claiming but demonstrating the many ways your investigation process has indeed been fair, you may not get the outcome you were hoping for internally, but you will avoid or minimize the long-term costs that a flawed investigation can and will entail.

"The more people feel certain of the outcome before findings are announced, the less likely the investigation was a fair and objective one."

THE FINDINGS

The more people feel certain of the outcome before findings are announced, the less likely the investigation was a fair and objective one. True, there are times when the matter under investigation is so egregious and the culpability so clear that most know what to expect, but in most cases the facts in dispute are unclear or complex enough that the parties should refrain from jumping to conclusions or signaling expected outcomes. If the outcome turns out otherwise, as happened in my case, the sense of outrage and betrayal can be great.

I was told George would be removed from the program if they found my allegation to be truthful. That didn't happen. The contradiction left me feeling betrayed and his continued presence frightened me. Now he would feel both wronged by me making the report—and vindicated. In the aftermath I felt even more powerless and afraid. As someone who has devoted her career to justice, the injustice of his egregious behavior without any meaningful penalty led me to seek justice. Ben was right when he told me I'd been assaulted. George had assaulted me. Later, Ben would say of the incident:

My concerns were nothing to do with the institution. They were to do with how you could not be further victimized in this prestigious environment. How could you recover from an assault, but still take part in the once-in-a-lifetime opportunity we were enjoying? I thought you should report this event because, as we discussed at the time, you should not be held back by what someone else did, and their continued presence was going to do that. The idea was not to escalate the situation, but to legitimize it and search for a route out that would benefit you.

When we went for a walk along the Charles River that afternoon, I remember thinking, I don't know Rebecca, I don't know George, but here I see trauma, I see physical evidence, I see someone reaching out for help. This has to be taken seriously, it has to be believed, it happened and it needs to be dealt with by HBS [Harvard Business School]. It had to be reported because it was your only route to freedom from the incident.[iv]

Feeling powerless in the institution, I reported the assault to the police and filed a formal Title IX complaint. As soon as the police contacted him for an interview, George voluntarily left the program and the state. I felt an immense sense of relief. The findings had left me feeling battered, but taking action left me feeling empowered and led to the outcome I had sought: I was safe.

As my own experience shows, some of the most volatile touchpoints happen while announcing the findings and recommendations that follow an investigation. When you acknowledge the damage someone has suffered and ask how to ensure they feel heard, you decrease the likelihood that findings and recommendations will cause further trauma. In your recommendations, include constructive actions to protect others from

---

[iv] Personal correspondence.

similar damage even if it means terminating a beloved employee or paying restitution to the victim. Instead of a huge disappointment or even re-traumatizing event, this touchpoint becomes a turning point toward healing and maintaining a positive organizational reputation.

"By making every touchpoint one that builds trust and confidence . . . , your institution is better served, your organizational culture is all the stronger, and your reputation is better protected."

Alternatively, the findings and recommendations could trivialize the damage someone suffered. A finding that confirms the wrongdoing but merely slaps the culpable party on the wrist can become a turning point leading straight to the press or courtroom. In my own case, learning that George had his classes and room changed but would remain down the hall from me translated to putting other students—and me—at risk. I felt safety for myself and other women in the program didn't matter. I had expected meaningful corrective action in line with the stated policies of the program. Instead, he got musical chairs. That was my own turning point toward taking further action.

No organization wants to deal with the conflicts, injuries, and damage. No organization wants to devote untold hours and dollars to investigating and resolving such matters, but all organizations do so at some point. When they do, if they understand the multiple points along the process that can become turning points, they are much less likely to suffer unnecessary time and expense correcting the problem or cleaning up the damage. By making every touchpoint one that builds trust and confidence rather than distrust, suspicion, and resistance to the process, your institution is better served, your organizational culture is all the stronger, and your reputation is better protected. Now, let's look more deeply at how to safeguard that reputation.

CHAPTER 6

SAFEGUARDING YOUR ORGANIZATION'S REPUTATION

There was a time when the worst that could happen to an organization was a scandal on the nightly news. Picture an attorney alongside a mother claiming the hospital in the background killed their baby; a resident in front of their building accusing the development company of building houses on a toxic landfill; or rejected students protesting because the university recruited wealthy, unqualified students in exchange for hefty donations. Such press conferences brought out every reporter within spitting distance to turn a once-manageable internal problem into a public scandal.

Today you don't need a press conference to damage an organization's reputation. One quick tweet or Facebook post can send your stock tumbling and your board of directors calling for heads to roll. Your immediate response to the problem will shape organizational culture, which, in turn, can influence your external reputation. You need to protect both.

As I've indicated, legal departments commonly deny accusations and, in many cases, discredit the accuser. By painting the accuser a liar, overly emotional, or just having an axe to grind, the organization hopes to manipulate public perception. Sounds like a useful tactic, but such a response can backfire for a couple of reasons.

"Attacking the reputation of a complainant to protect your own may come back to haunt you."

Attacking the reputation of a complainant to protect your own may come back to haunt you. Later, if evidence is produced that supports their claim, your organization not only appears heartless and aggressive for going after a victim, but will also be the one discredited. You'll have unjustly demonized a suffering party, damaged your own credibility by failing to appropriately respond to a claim, and likely caused even legitimate defenses to fall on deaf ears.

If the accuser has been traumatized by the response or non-response of your organization, public disparagement will intensify their determination to tell the world their experiences. It takes very little social media savvy to post damning photographs, share emails, or upload internal reports, all of which can rapidly undermine your defense.

When actress Rose McGowan accused Harvey Weinstein of raping her, the Hollywood producer hired Attorney Lisa Bloom as a consultant. Bloom, the daughter of renowned women's rights attorney, Gloria Allred, advised Weinstein to discredit McGowan.

She had no idea how badly her advice would backfire.

In a memo she wrote to Weinstein in 2016, Bloom suggested that she could plant articles in the press to portray the actress as "increasingly unglued so that when someone Googles her, this is what pops up and she's discredited." One year later, the day before *The New York Times* was set to publish a damning article exposing Weinstein's history of sexual predation and assault, Bloom and Weinstein attempted to discredit actress Ashley Judd and others bringing similar allegations. Bloom also contacted a journalist writing about Weinstein for *The New Yorker*, Ronan Farrow, enlisting the journalist to further discredit Rose McGowan.[i]

"The more aggressive you appear in public, the more sympathy may shift to the accusers and the more likely the accusers will react in kind."

Despite Bloom's efforts, the allegations of Judd, McGowan, and many other women regarding Weinstein's behavior were found to be credible. Not only did Bloom fail to counter the avalanche of accusations against Weinstein, but her actions were later documented by *NY Times* reporters Megan Twohey and Jodi Kantor in *She Said*,[ii] a book later made into a film. Weinstein

[i] Lisa Bloom offered to plant stories for Harvey Weinstein: book (page-six.com).

[ii] Kantor, Jodi and Megan Twohey (2019), *She Said: Breaking the Sexual Harassment Story That Helped Ignite a Movement*, New York: Penguin Press.

is currently serving twenty-three years in prison for rape, and Bloom's attacks on the victims severely damaged her reputation up to and including calls for her disbarment.

Does this mean you shouldn't defend your organization or your clients against accusations? Of course not. You have every right and responsibility to do so, and that includes the right to deny the accusation. What I'm suggesting is you temper any instinct to go on the attack, especially when drawing on the vast institutional weight of an organization against one or a few people. <u>The more aggressive you appear in public, the more sympathy may shift to the accusers and the more likely the accusers will react in kind.</u> They will take to social media. They will publish any threats or attacks on their character, and they will use the force of your attacks against them to topple you. So, what can you do to protect your organization from reputational damage?

In this chapter, we'll discuss how to:

- Work with your claimant in a non-adversarial manner.
- Identify steps to prevent further damage and potentially ward off a lawsuit.
- Establish a process that is clear and understandable to all concerned.
- Identify any "black holes" in your procedure that might not be serving your organization.
- Establish a process to monitor and follow up so no one "left in the dark" needs to take more serious measures.
- Train your frontline staff to conduct trauma-informed interviews.

THE COST OF A COVER-UP

Recall the case of Michigan State University (MSU) and its cover-up of Larry Nassar's crimes. Sadly, MSU is not alone in its misguided efforts to shield a serial sexual predator from accountability. When several women reported being sexually assaulted by Columbia University physician, OB/GYN Robert Hadden, M.D., the university opted to protect its reputation above past and future victims. As I write this, Columbia University has paid out nearly *a quarter billion dollars* to 226 women for its actions and failures to act. Their costs will likely continue to rise as more than 300 other women have since made credible reports of sexual assault by this same doctor.[iii]

[iii] Roush, Ty (2023), "Over 300 Alleged Sexual Abuse Victims Sue Columbia University—Claim Ex-Gynecologist Robert Hadden is 'Most Prolific' Predator in N.Y. History," *Forbes Magazine*, October 4. Available online at: Over 300 Alleged Sexual Abuse Victims Sue Columbia University—Claim Ex-Gynecologist Robert Hadden Is 'Most Prolific' Predator In N.Y. History (forbes.com).

───────

CASE STUDY
Columbia University and the Crimes of Dr. Hadden

Hadden joined the medical team at Columbia University in 1987, fresh out of medical school. Within five years, the university had been alerted to his crimes. The first was a sixteen-year-old pregnant girl who complained in 1992 that her exam was so rough she told him he was hurting her. The receptionist she spoke to about the incident handed her a sticky note with a phone number to call. She called the number several times before someone answered only to give her another number. This went on and on, from number to number, until she finally left a few voicemails. No one ever called her back.[iv]

Around this same time, another pregnant woman was molested by the doctor as an attendant in the room turned her back. The woman wrote two letters detailing the incident. One went to Columbia's risk management department and the other to the acting head of their OB/GYN department. Risk management never responded. The department head indicated he'd investigate. His investigation consisted merely of one question to the medical assistant. When the attendant claimed she saw nothing inappropriate during the exam, he made no further inquiries and had no further contact with the patient who made the report.

Columbia had no formal policy for reporting such behavior. In fact, it was later reported that the broader organizational culture ensured such complaints would not be well received. One former physician told reporters for New York Magazine *that "there was an ethos at Columbia of keeping quiet about anything that could reflect poorly on*

───────

iv Fortis, Bianca and Laura Biel (2023), "Protecting a Predator: How Columbia University Ignored Women, Undermined Prosecutors, and Allowed One of Its OB/GYNs to Abuse Hundreds of Patients," *New York Magazine,* September 11. Available online at: How Columbia University Protected Robert Hadden (nymag.com).

the university. 'If there was something that wasn't perfect, you better not talk about it,' she says. 'We don't want to ruin the reputation.'"[v]

Those perceptions had been echoed by nurses who witnessed the behavior but were afraid to speak out against a physician whose power and status was greater than those of a nurse. "I felt I didn't have a voice," one nurse said when interviewed for the New York Magazine article.

A medical assistant who worked with him at the time recalls questioning, along with her colleagues, why Hadden would often direct them to move on to the next patient before he had completed the exam in progress. Even so, after leaving her position, she returned in 1996 to see Hadden as a patient. She says that as she was lying on the examination table, Hadden rubbed his erect penis on her arm. Stunned and shaken, she told a receptionist that Hadden was a pervert. She recalls that the receptionist replied, "I know" and "I'm sorry."

In 2012, neither Columbia's legal department nor Hadden's supervisors could possibly deny the assaults. One of Hadden's patients, thirty-eight-year-old Laurie Kanyok, went to the police after a postpartum exam during which she felt Hadden's tongue on her vagina. The police took her seriously and arrested Hadden, but he was promptly released pending trial. Even after the university was informed of the arrest, they permitted him to continue seeing patients. Four days later, he assaulted another patient. He would assault a total of at least eight women during the five weeks the university allowed him to practice. It was only when he refused to comply with their internal investigation that he was suspended. Hadden, then in his sixties, "retired," and his patients were never notified of the reason for his departure. As for their "investigation," no one contacted the patient who'd filed the police report. Today, from their website, the

---

[v]   Fortis, Bianca and Laura Biel (2023), "Protecting a Predator: How Columbia University Ignored Women, Undermined Prosecutors, and Allowed One of Its OB/GYN's to Abuse Hundreds of Patients," *New York Magazine*, September 11. Available online at: How Columbia University Protected Robert Hadden (nymag.com).

university openly apologizes for the fact that it did not contact any of the doctor's patients about his crimes.[vi]

Once the police investigation against Hadden was underway, Columbia went to even greater lengths to avoid cooperating. They refused to comply with subpoenas and made no effort to admonish staff to safeguard evidence and refrain from deleting emails. When multiple women came forward with new reports, staff was instructed to contact the university's legal counsel whose concern was not justice for—but protection from—those women and their bad reports. They did not refer the matter to the Office of Professional Misconduct, as required by law, and failed to notify prosecutors of the additional witnesses. As a result, the case against Hadden was considered unwinnable. He was offered a plea deal requiring him to surrender his medical license and register as a sex offender, but served no jail time.

The plea deal did not make the matter go away. The university's failure to take responsibility and acknowledge the women's suffering grew into a massive problem. It grew exponentially when several of the women took their stories to the press. If the judicial system wasn't going to adequately address the matter, and the university wasn't going to even acknowledge it, maybe the media would.

The national attention that ensued led to an investigation by the Department of Justice, a twenty-year prison sentence for Hadden, and one of the costliest civil claims a university has ever paid out—with more likely to come. As New York Magazine put it, "One of the country's most acclaimed private universities was deeply involved in containing, deflecting, and distancing itself from the scandal at every step."

That pattern of deflection and failure to respond also contributed to the high number of women assaulted. In his twenty-five-year career with Columbia, Hadden saw an estimated 10,000 women as patients,[vii]

---

vi Columbia University website, www.cuimc.columbia.edu/rebuilding-trust.
vii Roush, Ty (2023), "Over 300 Alleged Sexual Abuse Victims Sue Columbia University—Claim Ex-Gynecologist Robert Hadden is 'Most Prolific' Predator in N.Y. History," *Forbes Magazine*, October 4. Available online at: Over 300

and he is alleged to have assaulted about 5 percent of his patients. Had he been stopped more than two decades prior when the university first became aware of his behavior, imagine how many women would have been protected from his sexual assault, and how much money Columbia could have saved.

———

"Foster a culture in which people don't fear coming forward . . . "

Let Columbia's costly lesson be your own—take complaints seriously. Establish a clear process for making reports. Ensure contact information is easy to find and that someone is available and ready to speak with the complainant immediately or very soon after the initial communication. Foster a culture in which people don't fear coming forward, and don't bury the complaint just because it could be stigmatizing. <u>It's the cover-up that destroys an institution's reputation</u> far more gravely than the actions of a single bad actor. Let's consider how you can avoid following in the footsteps of Columbia.

Alleged Sexual Abuse Victims Sue Columbia University—Claim Ex-Gynecologist Robert Hadden Is 'Most Prolific' Predator In N.Y. History (forbes.com).

PLANNING FOR PROBLEMS

When the first patient reported being abused by Hadden, university administrators did not take her report seriously. She was sixteen years old and had never had a gynecological exam. Perhaps they thought she was overreacting to a routine but uncomfortable procedure. As more rumors and reports came to their attention, they should have recognized the claim had teeth —that something was amiss. In safeguarding your organization's reputation, you might instinctively dismiss claims as being unfounded. That's why it's important to have a plan in place that treats every claim as potentially credible. Consider the consequences if you disregard it and the claim turns out to be true.

Once you realize a claim really does have teeth, what should you do? You know you probably have liability or will if you don't do something to correct the problem. Someone screwed up big time and their negligence is your liability; or someone crossed the line and abused or assaulted someone, violated the law, or otherwise acted in a manner that has not only exposed your organization to litigation, but if not handled properly, could lead to a PR disaster and the collapse or bankruptcy of your business. Columbia had no plan in place. You need a plan.

The best plan is one you put in place *before* the problem arises so that you limit the potential for litigation or bad press in the first place. While the majority of Hadden's crimes at Columbia happened before they had a plan, by the time I went to Harvard they had established plans and policies designed to safeguard both students and the institution. A hotline was posted for students to call if they felt harassed, threatened, or assaulted. They created an office with administrators responsible for just that sort of problem. They even published a detailed statement of their "Community Values," which made it clear that students were expected to create an environment of mutual trust and respect for their colleagues and faculty. Still, it all went so wrong right from the start.

> *"Your task is to turn a perceived 'problem' into an opportunity."*

The administrators I dealt with seemed as frustrated and felt as powerless as me. They recognized that they could do better, and that if they didn't do better, there would come a next time with another student and a potentially more damaging outcome. I'll tell you more about their solution and how they improved their process, but first, let's consider how you can avoid facing a similar problem by mitigating your damages and protecting your organization's reputation from the start.

Once an accusation of wrongdoing is made, it is natural to want to explain away problems that arise. You have invested so much in your organization, and your organization is probably wonderful. When someone brings to you an ugly problem, the last thing you want is to be identified with the incident they're describing. Columbia's self-protective actions ultimately tarnished their image and contributed to the preventable trauma and suffering of hundreds of women.

Your task is to turn a perceived "problem" into an opportunity. Perhaps their reputation would have taken a hit, but their prompt and proactive response could have not only mitigated that damage, but improved public perception as the people may have viewed the university as supporting women over reputation. They could have launched a publicity campaign showing their support for victims of sexual assault everywhere; thus, turning the "ugly" into something beautiful. But that's not what they did. If a hushed accusation proves legitimate, as most are, your early denials will be even more offensive as facts emerge.

ORGANIZATIONAL CULTURE

Organizational culture can be understood as ". . . the rules, values, beliefs, and philosophy that dictate team members' behavior in a company . . . , an established framework that guides workplace behavior." All businesses have their own organizational culture. In a poorly managed organizational culture, communication and productivity are disrupted. Conflicts and obstacles abound. Distrust permeates relationships. This leads to high turnover, unresolved systemic problems, and a culture of secrecy.

"To avoid internal chaos, implement a clear and understandable procedure with no secret 'back doors' or deliberate loopholes."

In more functional organizations, there is transparency at all levels. Rules and procedures are clearly articulated. Everyone associated with the organization feels respected and responsible for doing their part in promoting the organization's mission. Unfortunately, few organizations achieve this. Most sway somewhere between dysfunctional and functional. Without transparency the culture is weakened and susceptible to dysfunction, especially in the face of an accusation. It's no wonder, then, that anyone who reports a problem gets viewed as a problem themselves. It looks like they create a firestorm, but in reality they merely stepped onto a live landmine in a field of unresolved problems. Your best bet is to address the problem without creating new ones and causing internal chaos. To avoid internal chaos, implement a clear and understandable procedure with no secret "back doors" or deliberate loopholes. Clear policy is key to functionality in the midst of accusations and is a hallmark of a culture of transparency.

CREATING A CULTURE OF TRANSPARENCY

What does a "culture of transparency" mean? It means you do not hide problems but acknowledge and address them. You have open and honest discussions with your stakeholders and staff regarding risks, and you discuss findings with the relevant parties. Recall that nurses and staff at Columbia were well aware of Hadden's actions but they felt they couldn't speak up. They believed that the hierarchy of the hospital silenced them, and they wouldn't be believed if they spoke out against a physician. If you want to avoid going from bad to worse to potentially catastrophic, there needs to be transparency at all levels and safety for anyone who speaks up.

"If you want to avoid going from bad to worse to potentially catastrophic, there needs to be transparency at all levels and safety for anyone who speaks up."

As I write these words, a lawsuit is underway against a Yale University fertility clinic. Allegedly, a nurse was steeling fentanyl, a pain medication prescribed to patients following invasive fertility procedures, and replacing the pain meds with saline solution. Upon discovering the theft, the nurse was promptly fired and arrested, but in their efforts to keep the matter quiet, patients were never notified.

"When I learned years later that the excruciating pain I experienced was a direct result of the institution's failure to properly manage controlled substances, and that nobody on my care team or administrators at Yale had reached out to tell me about this, I felt betrayed," said plaintiff Kaitlin O'Connor, who is a practicing gynecologist.[viii]

It's that sense of betrayal that can intensify reactions. While you might feel that keeping something quiet will limit potential lawsuits, it can have the opposite effect if someone finds out, especially when the revelation comes by a news report or lawsuit. That's when the risk of a class action suit increases.

[viii] Stamp, Ellie (2023), "Lawsuit Alleges Nurse at Yale Fertility Clinic Swapped Pain Medication with Saline for Medical Procedures," www.wtnh.com, October 10,11. Available online at: Lawsuit alleges nurse at Yale fertility clinic swapped pain medication with saline for medical procedures (wtnh.com).

FOUR DOMAINS OF TRANSPARENCY

A report published by the National Patient Safety Foundation in 2015[ix] identified four domains of transparency within healthcare organizations:

1. Transparency between clinicians and patients.
2. Transparency among clinicians.
3. Transparency among institutions.
4. Public reporting of harmful events.

Whatever your organization, you likely have similar domains of transparency. There is transparency between staff and clients or customers; among staff members; among external colleagues and competitors; and in what you report to the public. Let's take a closer look at these domains.

TRANSPARENCY BETWEEN STAFF AND CLAIMANT

This level focuses on the person who comes to you with a complaint or concern, someone to whom you have a responsibility. Throughout this book I've been talking about this relationship and the importance of being open and honest with them. By acknowledging their concerns and focusing on getting at the truth instead of denying it happened, you lessen the likelihood of the problem escalating. In chapter eight, I will show you surprising data to support this point. Throughout the reporting process, the more you acknowledge the problem, have genuine and heartfelt discussions with the injured or aggrieved party,

---

[ix] The National Patient Safety Foundation's Lucien Leape Institute (2015). *Shining a Light: Safer Healthcare Through Transparency: Report of the Roundtable on Transparency.*

and explain the procedures and findings, the less stressful and consequential the problem will be for all.

"Communicate safety to all levels and at all levels of the reporting process . . . "

TRANSPARENCY AMONG STAFF

Among many professions, such as in medicine, there is a tendency to protect one's colleagues from accusations of wrong-doing. While I certainly do not advocate a culture of tattling, I do suggest that if there is a potential problem with a colleague that could cause harm or injury to someone, staff should feel free to speak up without retribution. If a physician is making multiple mistakes or abusing patients, his or her colleagues need to feel safe in bringing those incidents to the attention of administration *before* someone is seriously harmed. If a faculty member is known to be sexually harassing students, his or her colleagues need to know that saying something won't cost them their job or career. And if an attorney is considering misuse of clients' money, knowing that a proactive administration deals head-on with unethical and illegal conduct may prevent the misconduct altogether. Communicate safety to all levels and at all levels of the reporting process, and create protocols that facilitate safety as a goal.

TRANSPARENCY AMONG EXTERNAL COLLEAGUES AND COMPETITORS

It might seem contrary to all you've been taught, but as the National Patient Safety Foundation (NPSF) points out, sometimes it's important that competitors and colleagues from outside your organization know about a problem. Recall the many times Dr. Christopher Duntsch performed sadistically botched spinal surgeries on patients, yet hospital after hospital failed to reveal their concerns. If they'd done so, many lives would have been saved and critical injuries avoided. If a piece of equipment is known to be faulty and could potentially hurt someone, rather than keep your findings about it concealed, let your industry know so others don't buy the equipment. If there is any problem that others in your profession need to know about to avoid harming others, speak up![x]

TRANSPARENCY WITH THE PUBLIC

Finally, you need to be transparent with the public. When you are open with the public and enable people to make informed decisions, such as with surgical procedures, people are more likely to trust your organization. You are also more likely to address safety problems if you know that these problems will become public, possibly preventing incidents from happening in the first place.

Cultivating a culture of transparency is never easy because we like to protect ourselves from negative perceptions; but ultimately, the benefits outweigh the costs.

Columbia University now has on its website a page entitled, "Rebuilding Trust." Under the tab titled "Accountability" they state:

---

[x]   Columbia University website, www.cuimc.columbia.edu/rebuilding-trust.

While Hadden's misconduct, arrest, prosecution, and sentencing are widely known, and Columbia has announced its settlements with more than 220 survivors, Columbia has never directly reached out to Hadden's patients about his crimes. The actions now undertaken by the University are intended to correct this failure, repair the harm that has been done, and ensure we are fulfilling the high ideals of Columbia and the medical profession. Survivors of Hadden's abuse need to know they are not alone. We regret the impact of our handling of this matter on survivors and on our entire community. Earning our patients' trust is paramount to all we do.

Don't put your organization in the position of having to publish such an admission. Be transparent from the start.

In their 2015 report for the NPSF, authors noted four important reasons to cultivate a culture of transparency in medical institutions. Whether your organization provides healthcare or other services, these same benefits are likely to apply. Transparency facilitates:

1. Accountability.
2. Improved quality and safety.
3. Trust and ethical behavior within the organization.
4. Customer choice as customers can better evaluate their options, risks, and benefits.

To achieve such a culture of transparency requires a major shift in thinking from quashing complaints to addressing them. You must shift from retaliation against those who bring the problems to your attention, to punitive measures for those who are aware of problems but don't. A few steps is all you need to get started toward that end. A trauma-informed response will help you achieve that first domain of transparency for all whom you serve.

HAVE A FIRST CLEAR STEP

In the last chapter, I discussed how a well-designed process begins with a phone number and clear first steps. It was the ambiguity of these first steps that set off the problems I and Harvard administrators faced after reporting George's assault. To add to the problem, I later learned that the hotline I called <u>was</u> for all students. It was simply a training issue that led to my being told otherwise. As far as I knew, there was no other number for me to call. As patients of Dr. Hadden discovered, all the university could offer was a phone number scribbled on a sticky note, a number that got them nowhere. Don't let this simple step be one your organization overlooks.

TRAIN FRONTLINE STAFF IN TRAUMA-INFORMED RESPONSES

Frontline staff includes all managers and anyone who deals with human resources, client assistance, diversity and equity, public outreach, or any other person someone might report their concerns to. <u>Hold workshops and bring in experts who can explain how to listen and communicate with someone in a state of trauma.</u> Explain how such a person might present as unstable or not credible, not because they are mentally disturbed or lying but because they have been traumatized. Explain that if a person has been sexually harassed or assaulted, it's common to feel shame—and that shame does not mean they are responsible for what happened. Educate your staff on how the human brain derails in moments of trauma and what to expect from anyone in such a state, including confusion, disorganized memories, and acting impulsively.

ROLE PLAY TO REINFORCE TRAINING

It is not enough to tell your staff what to do. You also need to show them, and they need to practice. The best way to do that is through role-playing, preferably under the direction of someone trained in trauma-informed responses. Your staff members do not need to be trained counselors, but by training them in managing their social interactions with traumatized claimants, they will be better able to manage the investigation effectively. A traumatized person feels helpless. They've come to you for your help. With practice, the frontline representative in your organization will learn how to help the claimant feel empowered. Role-playing can also help staff learn to ask open-ended questions, listen without interrupting, and suppress any signs of judgment. By engaging in role-playing with staff, you won't walk away with the false confidence that they'll do a good job. You'll see for yourself whether they understand the process, and they will learn for themselves how to better interact with anyone who comes to them for help. This type of training is useful in dealing with clients, customers, and employees in general.

ELIMINATE "BLACK HOLES"

When I tried to call a hotline to report George's assault and was told (erroneously) that the number was not for students in my program, I'd stumbled into a "black hole." I existed in an area or class of people not included in the formal process and procedures. We seemingly existed in limbo while paying tuition, attending classes, and completing our program coursework. Consequently, there appeared to be no plan for students in the program who were abused, assaulted, harassed, discriminated against, or retaliated against. I found no clear resources, no numbers to call, no procedure to follow. No one even knew that this "black hole" existed until I reported an assault and was left in a predicament where I felt unsafe.

Such "black holes" are found in many organizations. Contract workers, for example, may not be your employees, but they are working for you. While on your clock, on your property, or acting in any way as an agent or client of your organization, you are responsible even if you haven't made provision for them in the case of an incident.

"It's rare that a false accusation of wrongdoing is made against an organization."

Another "black hole" I encountered at Harvard was the "Community Values." These values were great but secondary to the federal guidelines of Title IX they had to comply with in taking any action. The collision between internal "community values" and state or federal laws is common. You may draft a Code of Conduct and have everyone sign it, and then find that when a discrimination claim is made your Code of Conduct is worth little. What matters are federal laws pertaining to discrimination. Yet these gaps between laws and organizational policies are common. At best, when an organization suddenly becomes aware of how their policies might conflict with the law, makeshift procedures are slapped together to force legal compliance while the injured party feels betrayed because the policies aren't being honored. Don't wait for the problem to arise. Identify anyone who could potentially bring a legal action against your organization. Review your reporting process to eliminate "black holes". Make sure everyone is covered and that your policy aligns with local and federal laws.

COOPERATE WITH THE CLAIMANT

Make it a priority to cooperate with the claimant from beginning to end. It's rare that a false accusation of wrongdoing is made against an organization. There may be disputes over some of the facts or details, and there may be differences in how culpability is assigned, but most people who come forward alleging they have been injured will feel genuinely wronged. I know I certainly did.

Once George had withdrawn from the program, I felt relieved. Yet, because he left the program, there was no adjudication. I later received a letter from the Title IX office telling me that my complaint had been dismissed. Thus, there was no official record of George's assault.

Moreover, after I graduated from the program I learned of his intention to reapply for admission in the program, and Harvard was going to "investigate" before making an admissions decision. This meant they would speak to him but not reopen the Title IX investigation. It was then that I reached out to an administrator in human resources to learn the status of that investigation. I was immediately frustrated by her demeanor. She seemed unwilling to tell me much of anything. Having graduated, I felt as if I was no longer viewed as relevant. The whole matter had produced a turmoil of emotions from the beginning and made it more difficult to get through the program. My confidence was shaken, so reaching out to HR was not a step I wanted to take but no one was telling me anything. I needed reassurance that George was not going to be allowed to come back to the program to do this to another unsuspecting student. I also needed some basic human kindness after all I'd been through.

Instead, I felt like an annoyance at best, a problem at worst. She refused to tell me the outcome of the investigation. The way she handled the issue further inflamed me and made me want to go public. Even though Harvard itself did not assault me, they were responsible for providing a safe learning environment for their students. When I went to administrators with my concerns seeking a proactive response, I believe they wanted to give one. But when they were unable, they became more responsible for the bad outcome. I felt powerless in the process. To my mind, taking further action was a way to regain the power George seized the moment he held me in his grip and wouldn't let me go. Now, as I communicated with the woman from HR, instead of feeling helped, I felt worse.

"Dear Rebecca," she wrote, "An overview of our Executive Education Community Values process can be found here," and she included a link to the "Community Values" they had already determined were superseded by Title IX. "Please note that our review of this complaint has concluded, and the disclosure of the final results is governed by federal law (FERPA)."

That was the entirety of her response to me. It was a non-response that essentially said she wasn't going to tell me anything because George's admission was not my business under his privacy rights guaranteed by FERPA. As a lawyer, I knew those privacy rights also applied to me. I had access to any records pertaining to me, and hence, I had a right to answers. So, I made some noise. I replied by pointing out my legal rights to the records. It was then that I discovered through an informal communication that his application for readmission had been denied.

After I graduated from the Advanced Management Program and returned to practice law in Michigan, I was in communication with administrators at Harvard Business School (HBS) who had evaluated my concerns. These concerns included how the manner had been handled—from having no hotline to their not removing George from classes, keeping him in the same housing unit, and issuing *me* a no-contact order, as if to suggest that I was as culpable as him. When I heard he'd applied for readmission, I felt even more upset. In my view, nothing had been done to make the environment safer, but everything seemed to protect George, even enabling him to return to potentially harm other students.

I'm sure the university did become greatly concerned that their (in)actions could impact future attendance or even harm its reputation. That was something they certainly wanted to avoid. They were likely also concerned that I would be vocal in the press, which could adversely impact the already low number of women participating in the program. Fortunately, by working together we were eventually able to transform a bad outcome into a favorable one.

"When I saw that they were genuinely trying to help me and protect others from similar abuse, I no longer felt adversarial."

My contacts at HBS invited me back out to Cambridge to meet with additional administrators where I shared my recommendations for procedures to protect the institution and its students. Many of the steps I've discussed in this book are those that I recommended to Harvard. By involving me in the process, what began as a contentious battle for personal self-protection became a pivotal encounter that positively changed procedures and resulted in a more effective reporting process. Being involved in these improvements also shifted me from being re-traumatized to feeling supported, heard, and helped. I felt that I was able to make the situation better for the next person. When I saw that they were genuinely trying to help me and protect others from similar abuse, I no longer felt adversarial. What could have become a public debacle instead became a constructive experience for us all.

In my case, healing came at the far end of the process after the findings were made, after I'd graduated and left the program, and after I returned to help administrators learn to respond better and more humanely. Don't wait until the process is concluded to figure out what went wrong and how you could have done better. Start at the beginning. Cooperate through to the end.

WHAT DO THEY WANT

From the very first touchpoint, the person reporting the problem needs to feel they have been heard. They need to clearly understand what will happen next in the process, and to be asked what they want or need to happen to help make them whole again. A family who has lost a child to medical malpractice will never "be made whole," but they will feel less shattered and enraged if they feel their concerns are being fairly and honestly examined.

"From the very first touchpoint, the person reporting the problem needs to feel they have been heard."

In the Hulu series, *Fleishman is in Trouble,* there is a scene in which the protagonist, a physician, snaps at the surviving spouse of a patient who has died. The physician feels the death was unfortunate but unpreventable, while the surviving spouse feels betrayed because the physician had previously expressed so much confidence in the procedure. With his mind on other matters, the otherwise-compassionate physician treats the grieving spouse badly. Later, the physician reflects on the trauma the spouse is experiencing and awkwardly shares a compassionate hug. Sometimes all a person *wants* is compassion. Left unsaid but expressed in the actions of the characters is the power of a moment like that to prevent the malpractice suit so feared by the physician.

As simple as it may sound, it is uncommon for an administrator to ask an injured party how they can help. In many cases, all someone wants is a conversation with the person they view as responsible. They might be satisfied with an apology or they may want protection. Even monetary requests can be comparatively minimal, initially. They may seek no more than reimbursement for damages—damages that may seem negligible but are symbolic to someone who feels they've had to pay monetary costs for something someone else caused them. At the very least, you are in a position to listen to them.

Sarah's Realtor

Sarah Mitchell discovered that her realtor had forged her name on several documents related to a pending home sale. Those forgeries lost her a higher-paying sale in favor of the realtor's clients who ultimately bowed out at the last minute, forcing Sarah to relocate to a new city for work while her house remained on the market. Moreover, previous real estate purchases and sales with this same realtor had been suspicious and cost her money when the realtor advised her not to sell to certain potential buyers. Sarah was certain that, in every instance, the realtor had not only forged her signature but was manipulating the sale process, showing favor to her own buyer clients to secure commission on both ends of the sale. This scheme ultimately stole profits from the client while doubling the realtor's money.

When Sarah met with the realtor's employer, she showed him photos of the forged signatures and told him of her resultant financial losses. The broker could have easily dismissed Sarah, denied culpability, hoped she would go away, or insisted she had made it all up. Instead, he asked, "What would you like us to do?"

Sarah didn't want to fight. Yes, she wanted the realtor fired and stripped of her license, but that was the broker's battle to wage, she reasoned. She wanted to be compensated for the financial losses from previous sales. She also asked the company to issue her a no-interest loan to cover her down payment on the new house, which would be paid back when the real estate company sold her house through another agent.

Without hesitation, the realtor wrote the check and the matter was resolved. Sarah closed on her new house, eventually sold the former house, and repaid the advance given by the real estate company. What could have led to costly litigation and reputational damage was quietly and peaceably resolved because someone asked her what she wanted.

———

One caveat: "How can I help you?" always goes further than, "You're crazy, get out of here," but don't make false promises. Be clear about what you can or cannot do while keeping in mind that someone has come to you for help, not for battle.

SIMPLE PROCEDURES TO MITIGATE DAMAGE

To ensure that everyone involved feels they have been treated fairly, and to minimize unnecessary escalation of an otherwise resolvable issue, ensure that every investigation does the following:

Provide the main parties with resources. Part of helping is providing access to resources, both within your organization and beyond. Most importantly, be clear about who to call from the onset. If the abusive actions continue, who do they contact? What if they feel someone has retaliated or rumors have begun to swirl? Who needs to know and what kind of help is available? Be sure they have names, phone numbers, and locations for anyone and any services they may need.

Do you offer counseling services? Financial assistance? Housing? If a person has lost income or become homeless because of the injury or loss they've suffered, perhaps you have resources available within your organization to help them. In most cases, the resources they need are related to mental health counseling, grief counseling, or PTSD. By having these resources readily available and sharing them from the start, you will minimize the damage. Are there national or community resources that may help them, such as support groups? Know what they need to begin the healing process and provide them with those resources.

Clarify the procedure. Remember that a traumatized brain is easily confused. Someone coming to you for help is not going to understand your institutional process or procedures. They're likely to have their own idea of how you should handle the matter. "Just kick them out" or "just write them a check" is probably not an option.

Ask them what they want. Involve them in the process. There is always a process involved, and the more they understand that process, the better. Have available a printout mapping the procedures. Keep in mind that they may not have the capacity to understand all that is available to them in the moment, so it is helpful to send them off with resources they can read or view when alone.

Be sure the person making the report leaves feeling heard, not defensive. The person should understand that they will be asked difficult questions but should never feel doubted or interrogated. One of the most common responses Dr. Hadden's victimized patients had was that no one so much as acknowledged their existence after they'd reported his behavior. Such a disregard for the legitimacy of their claim would leave anyone feeling defensive and possibly even re-traumatized. <u>Take full advantage of every touchpoint to ease anxieties.</u> Make the person be and feel heard to diminish the likelihood that they leave the meeting feeling defensive and wanting to take more severe action against your organization.

Be sure that everyone interviewed understands the nature of the accusation. Although they do not need to know all the details, the more everyone understands the nature of the investigation, the less uncertainty and anxiety they will feel, and the less likely they'll be to escalate the problem.

Gather more rather than less evidence. Ask each witness, including the accused, if they have any evidence to support their own claims and statements. <u>Never refuse evidence</u> and always review it objectively.

Request witnesses. Similarly, ask any involved parties for a list of witnesses they suggest for the investigation. Always follow up by contacting those potential witnesses. When you do, be sensitive to the witnesses' potential fear of speaking freely, for instance, if there are power imbalances between them and the accused or accuser. Interact with <u>everyone</u> using trauma-informed response methods.

Never threaten. Do not threaten or imply to any claimant, accused, or witness that anyone will be penalized in any way if the investigation's findings don't support what has been testified to or alleged. If they refuse to cooperate, document that refusal and reach out to them again after you've spoken with more people. Often people refuse to cooperate because they *do* know something, but they fear for their job, or in some way their security and safety.

Listen. Listen and ask follow-up questions. It's surprising how many investigations are conducted by people who interrupt or dismiss what a witness tells them. They ask few follow-up questions or none, and often only ask a few predetermined questions as if ticking off a list of questions to ask before dismissing the witness. Investigators should be trained to listen and direct the dialogue toward facts, not allowing the conversation to ramble or produce only selected responses toward a predetermined conclusion.

Update often. Provide timely and informative updates to the primary parties involved and answer their questions as much as possible. Flippant responses such as, "We'll determine the timeline," or "When our report is complete, we'll send you a copy," effectively state, "Your stress doesn't matter, and what we're doing is none of your business." That's the response that increases the odds of your claimant making noise. Make them feel supported throughout the process. That doesn't mean the investigation has to be biased. It means you recognize that the process is extremely stressful for them.

Assign someone to follow up. Just as you need to be clear about the resources available to claimants, be sure someone is assigned to follow up throughout the process. By following up, I don't mean keep an eye on the claimant. Appoint a designated administrator as your liaison to make sure the process is clearly articulated. Check in periodically with staff and the claimant to ensure that the matter is being appropriately addressed. Inquire as to how the claimant is feeling and if anything more can be done. <u>Select someone with excellent interpersonal skills that will enable them to work well with both accuser and accused</u>. Be sure they are good listeners, diplomatic, proactive, and empathetic. Have them ensure that any commitments or assurances are kept.

The claimant should feel safe expressing any concerns with any person they encounter, but especially this key point of contact. And it's vital that this liaison feels free to express any concerns to management about how the process is going. Providing this level of service does not mean you are caving into a claimant's demands. It means you are protecting your organization by respecting the claimant, recognizing his or her humanity and trauma, and remaining alert to any potential problems that could lead to litigation down the line.

Ask for feedback. At some point, the process will conclude. Feedback from those involved can provide useful information for improving responses and potentially prevent costly lawsuits or PR issues in the future. Have your client care coordinator check in to determine how staff treated the person bringing the complaint. We have this role in my organization, and we've found it invaluable in providing us with the feedback we need to continually improve our process.

Reach your conclusions in a timely manner. An investigation that drags on for months, sometimes even years, is typically not a professional investigation. You do not have to hold congressional hearings to determine whether someone in your charge has violated policies, ethics, or the law. <u>The longer an investigation continues the more rumors will fly, and the more likely the matter will be publicized first on social media and possibly in the mainstream media</u>. <u>This causes anxieties to rise, which often leads directly to lawsuits.</u>

At the same time, if the investigation is too quick, it will be clear that it was not thorough. Of course, there are some accusations that are so serious that the initial investigation must be swift to determine the level of danger so you can take quick action in a dire situation. The important thing is to do the best investigation possible to first determine if someone must be immediately removed from the environment, and then follow up with a more thorough investigation to determine the facts with more clarity and detail.

". . . when someone says they have been harmed by your organization or one of its agents, what follows [can be] a partnership that uses the problem as a springboard for opportunity to protect people and your institution."

Every organization has areas where procedures can be

improved, even the most state-of-the-art and well-known world-wide institutions like Harvard. Though eventually Columbia created procedures for effective reporting, when reporters from *New York Magazine* asked staff about these procedures, staff members were unaware of them. I hope you can see the benefits of clear and effective procedures and a trauma-informed response.

Finally, remember that when someone says they have been harmed by your organization or one of its agents, what follows does not need to be adversarial but can instead be a partnership that uses the problem as a springboard for opportunity to protect people and your institution. Let's take a look at how you can do that, even when someone comes to you screaming and threatening to sue.

CHAPTER 7
SEEING COMPLAINTS AS OPPORTUNITIES

How can you turn a seemingly adversarial conflict into a constructive partnership? I've said before that if someone comes to you with a grievance you should see it as an opportunity, but those words can ring hollow when you're faced with a potentially costly, embarrassing accusation. To make matters worse, sometimes the person making the claim is problematic. You may not like, trust, or believe them, but there are no perfect victims. As an executive charged with protecting your organization, your first responsibility is to the organization —which is best served by eliminating hostilities and creating a constructive partnership. How can you create that out of the mess that's been laid at your feet?

First, don't see the complaint as a threat but an opportunity to potentially eliminate or reduce future risks and bigger problems. When you respond this way, you foster a culture that honors people's concerns and creates a safe space for information to reach you. Embrace your role as a creator of culture. You are not only responsible for protecting your organization, but also for exemplifying how your organization responds to problems and protects its people. In other words, culture begins with you. You have more power than you may realize in shaping your organization from the inside out.

". . . while trying to quash a potential legal claim does not always make the problem go away, an organizational culture that effectively addresses the problem—can. *"*

Over ten years ago, our firm made a great decision to give our staff training and additional tools to continue expanding upon our amazing culture as we grew. Anese Cavanaugh is a well-known speaker, strategist, and advisor to leaders and organizations worldwide. In her book, *Contagious Culture,*[i] Cavanaugh suggests that whatever your role in an organization, you have more control than you realize over how that organization operates just by your response to challenges. With focus on healthy leadership and cultural skills, she held deep-dive workshops with teams and one-on-one meetings with leadership. Working with Anese was quite impactful. Her material emphasizes the power of healthy organizational culture, which applies here because while trying to quash a potential legal claim does not always make the problem go away, an organizational culture that effectively addresses the problem—*can*. In the first place, culture determines the types of messes you're likely to

---

[i]   Cavanaugh, Anese (2015), *Contagious Culture: Show Up, Set the Tone, and Intentionally Create an Organization That Thrives.* McGraw Hill.

encounter, and after that, informs people of how they should respond to those messes.

ASSUME GOOD INTENTIONS

Beginning with doubt and suspicion can cause you to ignore the little red flags that precede the red smoke signal people send once they have had enough. We live in a world filled with trickery and deceit. As a lawyer, I know people readily lie, betray, and act in their own self-interest, but I also know that there is a distinction between being judicious in evaluating people and being cynical by presuming the worst. When we do presume the worst in others, we come off aggressive and self-protective. People adapt to our projected suspicions by telling us what we want to hear and by withholding information. This only hinders investigations.

"If an organization exposes or brings undue shame on the accused, the accused may well return the favor."

It may be hard to trust that the people we encounter have good intentions, but really, you're not so much trusting the people as you're trusting the process. Take the radical step of presuming people have the best intentions. If they are being deceptive or their story has holes in it, your honest and thorough examination of the problem will bring reality to light. Most often, the person coming forward is alerting you to a problem and hoping you'll help. They generally believe that by speaking up they are doing you a service often at personal risk to themselves.

What about the accused? I would never suggest that George had good intentions when he assaulted me, nor when he partially admitted what he had done and cooperated with the school's investigation. Still, I have no doubt that he viewed himself as a man of good intentions. When we approach people with this understanding, we more easily gain the cooperation and trust that make truthful disclosures more likely. Furthermore, we create a culture that demonstrates mutual respect. If an organization exposes or brings undue shame on the accused, the accused may well return the favor. <u>Treating the accused as inherently bad will not persuade them to cooperate. It will shut them down just as it would shut down the claimant.</u>

Most importantly, your response to the claimant, the accused, and everyone involved demonstrates to the organization how your culture responds to challenges. Restrain biases for or against the accused to show that, in your culture, people remain innocent until proven guilty. This not only alleviates the pressure on those accused but also on people coming forward who don't necessarily mean to "make trouble." Use the complaint as an opportunity to demonstrate a culture of respect by protecting and honoring all parties involved. Within a culture of respect, future concerns are more likely to be expressed long before molehills become mountains.

CREATE A COOPERATIVE EXPERIENCE

Understand that while every party involved wants to protect themselves, they also want to work *with* you. By viewing all involved parties as a member of your team, regardless of their role, you are better positioned to create a cooperative experience for everyone involved.

If we're going to begin by assuming good intentions and trust the process, we'll need a process we can trust. How do you do this?

- **Be curious.** Listen actively. Don't interrupt. Ask open-ended questions. Ask them what they want and how you can help. Whether it's the claimant, the accused, the human resources rep, crisis counselor—anyone and everyone with whom you interact—avoid assumptions. Be curious enough to find out what is working and not working for them. Find out the outcome they desire and how you can help them achieve that. Staying curious will help you discern more and draw more accurate conclusions.
- **Identify biases.** Each person's belief system shapes the reporting and investigative process. As you talk with each person, their underlying assumptions are revealed. Do they tend to sympathize with the accuser or the accused? Do you perceive anything hindering their objectivity? Have they made judgments that may affect how they proceed? Be aware of your own underlying beliefs, preferences, or assumptions and take care not to impart those during your process. Be vigilant to detect anything that jeopardizes objectivity.
- **Reassure.** Whenever an interaction ends with one party feeling shut off or cut off, more problems emerge. Make sure each person you interact with leaves feeling heard and involved in the process, and reassure them that you value their cooperation.
- **Clearly define each person's role.** Even if someone's role in the investigation is minor, be sure they understand the importance and the limitations to that

role. You neither want them interjecting in matters beyond their responsibility or interests, nor withholding because they feel their input is out of place. Be ready to clearly and respectfully clarify their role as needed throughout the process.

- **Treat everyone as equally deserving of respect.** How can you resolve this conflict in a manner that doesn't dehumanize anyone and respects all people involved? How can you respond to the allegation in a manner that respects the humanity of the claimant? How can you take the next step in a manner that recognizes that someone feels harmed? You don't know all the facts, but you want to protect your organization's legal interests. By asking these questions of yourself, you stand a better chance of avoiding a lawsuit—and even if a lawsuit does come your way, you're more likely to protect the reputation of your organization and minimize the fallout within.

Instead of viewing your impact as limited to just quashing the allegation and keeping your people in line, you can create an organizational culture that over time reduces incidences and reports of wrongdoing. You will have fewer reports not because people keep their mouths shut, but because the culture itself takes concerns seriously, searches out matters when brought to light, and therefore minimizes the likelihood of people being harmed in the first place. In the event someone is harmed, the response is a constructive one that minimizes the potential for going to court.

"When abuses are less likely to be reported, abusers are empowered . . . , which in turn increases your likelihood of a more serious incident.

AVOID CREATING A TOXIC WORK CULTURE

The more hostile an internal investigative process, the more toxic the workplace culture. When your investigative process is known to be toxic and even hostile to complainants, people tend to keep their mouths shut. They may talk to each other rather than anyone in authority, thus creating a culture of gossip. When abuses are less likely to be reported, abusers are empowered because they know they can get away with inappropriate behavior, which in turn increases your likelihood of a more serious incident.

Furthermore, a toxic culture prevents witnesses from coming forward. Anese Cavanaugh notes that people need to feel safe to give honest feedback, tell the truth, admit to what they don't know, and openly disagree. Favoritism, for example, towards more powerful individuals in an organization can be a prime ingredient for toxic culture. If your organization tends to cover for people higher on the totem pole, you can be sure the others are aware of it, and this opens the door for a grand parade of toxic trends in an institution.

To assess your own organization, consider: If your supervisor was accused, might the investigation be steered more or less favorably simply because of their rank or power? Would the evidence be objectively evaluated? Would *you* feel inclined to believe or disbelieve a claim simply because of your relationship to the one accused?

What if the claimant has no power? Would a poor, uneducated woman who lost her baby due to possible medical negligence receive the same respect as a wealthy, educated woman with the same set of facts? How power influences communication determines whether the organization is toxic or relatively healthy. To guard against harmful toxicity in your organizational culture:

- **Assess the organizational structure.** Determine who reports to whom and how power is allocated. Is one person assuming all the power and controlling the flow of information, while others are prevented from open communication? You may not be able to change that structure, but your awareness of it will help you make an assessment and proceed with your eyes wide open.
- **Treat every rank and role equally.** Whether a janitor, security guard, chief surgeon of your hospital, COO or CEO, claimant, accused, or witness, ensure that each feels equally respected and recognized.
- **Be honest.** Just as you ensure that everyone feels heard when they come to you with a problem, ensure that you speak to them truthfully. Don't lie to them. Don't make promises you can't keep and keep the promises you make. Be accountable and hold others accountable. If you don't, a small incident could erupt into a much greater offense simply because your words did not align with your actions.
- **Be clear about expectations.** This includes what you expect from others and what they can expect from you. Remember that ambiguity breeds rumors and

anxiety. Just as raising a well-adjusted child means giving them clear rules about how they're expected to behave and enforcing those rules consistently, creating a well-adjusted organizational culture removes ambiguity and follows through on set expectations according to its core values.

- **Create a sense of safety.** Whether it's your own office, HR, or an Office of Equity and Diversity that is charged with investigating internal complaints, be sure that those who come to the office feel safe both entering and leaving. Don't threaten, don't intimidate, and don't bribe or otherwise manipulate anyone into changing what they came to you to say. Begin and end with fostering a sense of safety throughout your organization.

Everyone wants to feel they have power over their own lives, but when we've been injured we inevitably feel a loss of that power which, in turn, causes us to feel anxious. Building a safe, nontoxic organizational culture where people feel free to share their negative experiences, you may initially find you have more problems than ever, but this is only because what was once hidden is now coming to light. Over time, those who cause the problems will be weeded out and conflicts will be more readily resolved with less cost and less fallout. Moreover, by spotting and addressing the problems early, they won't get bigger. Let's consider the story of Victor Martinelli, a chef hired by an up-and-coming restaurant in a major west coast city.

Case Study
Victor Martinelli

When Rob and Wayne opened their high-end restaurant in a major metropolis, they knew they had a potential hit. They had an excellent location, limited competition, and years of experience in business and entrepreneurship. The one thing they lacked was an outstanding chef. Then, Victor Martinelli walked through the door.

Martinelli looked the part of the brilliant chef. Brooding, moody, ambitious, and with a gift of gab, he charmed the two men for hours telling of his love of food, his world travels as a student at the top cooking schools, and two decades working his way up the ladder to executive chef for one of the most respected hotel chains in the nation. Martinelli was just what they were looking for. His ideas for the menu were new and exciting, his enthusiasm high, and his salary—for a chef of such stature—reasonable. They wanted him immediately. There was only one catch. He lived on the other side of the country and needed a sizeable advance to make the move.

They paid it.

When he arrived, they encountered another problem. Upon relocating, it appeared his estranged wife had tossed him out of the house, stolen his car, and seized his bank accounts. He would need an additional advance just to get settled.

They paid it.

I think you can see where this story is going. Sure enough, the restaurant opened to great excitement. In no time, the restaurant was packed with hungry customers ready to pay a premium to dine there, but one after another, problems arose. The food turned out to be of lower standard than they'd expected. The service was poor, with diners waiting too long to get their food. Expenses climbed as the chef seemed only to purchase exorbitantly priced ingredients.

When a prep cook reported to the owners her suspicion that Martinelli wasn't really a chef, they fired her. "A prep cook," Rob screamed, "should know her place and not question her supervisor's expertise." He dug in his heels and backed Martinelli. After all, it wasn't the chef's fault his staff was so incompetent. They just needed a new staff.

Of course, that would cost more money, but the chef assured them he could bring in his former staff from the hotel. It would just take more money, some of it in cash for his crew to be paid under the table.

They paid it.

Meanwhile, the prep cook did what Rob and Wayne had not done. She contacted the hotel where he supposedly worked, the schools he'd supposedly attended, and the "estranged wife" who supposedly stole his car. He'd never worked at the hotel, nor attended the cooking schools, nor been married, and the car had never been his because he had stolen it. Children he claimed were his were photos he'd stolen from the woman he'd falsely claimed was his estranged wife. It turns out someone else had been conned out of thousands by the same man, and had hired a private detective who found this "chef" had a long history of stealing money and conning others. He had briefly served as a line cook at a family restaurant until he was fired for incompetence. That was the extent of his experience in restaurants.

When the prep cook returned to the restaurant to tell Rob and Wayne of her findings, hoping they'd rehire her, they read the report with concern but sent her away, telling no one of what they'd just learned. Their reasoning? By that time, they had given him so much money they feared the only way to cut their losses was to keep him on until he worked off his debt.

Did it work?

Quite the opposite. The "crew" he supposedly had hired from his former restaurant were people he found locally who had minimal food experience. He skimmed money by charging for high-priced ingredients and buying the cheapest ones. He presided over a New Year's Eve fiasco *that was so badly executed, every patron in the restaurant stormed out, the local newspaper wrote a scathing review, and it was years before they recouped their losses. They were fortunate they didn't need to close.*

———

BIASES, PREJUDGMENTS, AND COGNITIVE DISSONANCE

Refusing to hear the concerns of a "lowly" prep cook cost the owners a fortune. Because she was of low status in the restaurant, they didn't want to hear what she had to say. Because they had invested so much money in the "chef," they didn't want to admit they'd been duped so they gave him even more money—a perfect example of cognitive dissonance. When we make a mistake, rather than admit it, we often double down and become even more convinced we were right. Con artists count on cognitive dissonance to continue extracting money from their prey.

You may not deal with many con artists along the way, but in your efforts to protect your organization you can fall victim to cognitive dissonance and not see the evidence that is before you. Had they seized the prep cook's initial complaints as an opportunity, they could have prevented the debacle that followed. If you ignore the alarm like Rob and Wayne did, you could see the problem grow from bad to worse.

Often, the damage is far greater than a disastrous meal. Recall in chapter three I discussed the case of Dr. Christopher Duntsch, the surgeon sentenced to prison for the egregious surgeries he performed on unsuspecting patients' spines. Several people knew he was not just incompetent—he was intentionally killing and crippling his patients. Yet, people were afraid to speak up even after he'd left one hospital for another. Information was withheld. How was that possible?

"... failing to listen to someone bringing a problem to your attention can cost you far more than addressing the problem in the first place."

Fear is a powerful motivating factor and, all too often, it motivates people to fall silent. Fear of retaliation, being reprimanded, not believed, or wasting time and effort can not only silence reports but, in turn, allow the problem to get bigger.

We like to believe that the people we trust will protect us. In the story of Larry Nassar, we see the problem of inherent bias. He could have been stopped earlier before he abused so many young women, but he was a trusted doctor. When early reports of his abuse began to surface, some did nothing because they were influenced by his position. They couldn't imagine such a renowned physician would hurt others.

FEAR

Perhaps the greatest obstacles to turning complaints into opportunities include fear of speaking up only to face backlash, and fear of admitting error. These two fears often cost organizations dearly because foreseeable problems are covered up or left unaddressed, allowing situations to worsen and even lead to criminal charges. In Seattle, Washington, for example, the owner of a construction company was sentenced to forty-five days in jail and eighteen months' probation for manslaughter after he failed to provide adequate safety measures for his workers, leading to the death of a thirty-six-year-old man who was buried alive when a trench he was digging collapsed.[ii] Because the owner of the company had been cited for willfully failing to address workplace hazards, he not only ended up with a felony conviction and jailtime, but his company was also fined $25,000, they were prohibited from working on certain types of projects, and they were found civilly liable for causing the death of an employee. Such criminal charges are expected to rise as courts in states such as Washington have found that owners can be held criminally liable for deaths caused in connection with their work. Thus, failing to listen to someone bringing a problem to your attention can cost you far more than addressing the problem in the first place.

Sometimes the problem you need to address isn't brought to you by a single person but a pattern you've chosen to ignore. I'm not talking of just the cases of Dr. Christopher Duntsch, whose surgical assaults were apparent to his employers for years. There are times when organizations choose to settle costly lawsuits or even go to court for repetitive problems because they think litigation is cheaper than fixing the problem, but even in those cases the result is often far more costly than anticipated.

[ii] Historic decision: Employer faces jail time for worker's death in trench collapse – KIRO 7 News Seattle; Construction Company Owner Sentenced Criminally for 2016 Workplace Death - The Seattle Medium.

CASE STUDY
7-Eleven Storefronts

Take the case of the popular convenience store chain, 7-Eleven. You have probably noticed the 7-Eleven stores commonly include an adjacent parking lot so that cars are directly in front of the glass windows. What you may not know is that every day somewhere in the United States someone drives straight into those storefronts, either intentionally or accidentally. That's just at 7-Elevens. According to the Storefront Safety Council, more than one hundred times a day someone drives into a building somewhere in the United States, leading to over 16,000 injuries annually and 2,600 deaths.[iii] Such crashes are often avoided by installing simple steel posts that cost a mere $800. Owners and managers of 7-Eleven franchises should have been well aware of the danger and the solution, but despite the multiple crashes—and lawsuits—many stores have done nothing to address the problem.

One 7-Eleven ignored the pattern. One day a man got into his car in front of that 7-Eleven and, not realizing his car was in drive rather than reverse, hit the accelerator and drove straight through the glass storefront. That day, another man who stopped into the store for a cup of coffee lost both his legs. Failure to fix the problem cost the plaintiff something he can't get back. It also cost 7-Eleven a $91 million settlement,[iv] a far cry from the initial $800 expense. It pays to listen when you're made aware of problems even if doing so might cost you in the short term.

---

iii ABOUT | Store Front Safety Council
iv How the 7-Eleven Storefront Crash Settlement Highlights the Importance of Retail Safety and Perimeter Security - Security Industry Association.

It's remarkable how many lawsuits can be avoided just by listening. When a storage facility's lock was somehow broken, my loved one's treasured 1969 Camaro was stolen. He'd owned the car since he was a teenager. The loss was heartbreaking, but at least the storage facility was insured. When he contacted the insurance adjuster to recover the out-of-pocket expenses to recover the car, the adjuster accused him of being "in on" the theft and committing fraud!

You may think such accusations are rare, but they are all too common. By accusing someone of committing a crime when they ask to be compensated for damages they've suffered, they're hoping the problem goes away. "Turning the tables" on the complainant puts them on the defensive. It might intimidate them enough to step back for fear of being charged with a crime, but this tactic also backfires because no one who is innocent wants to put up with being accused of a crime. All he'd wanted was reasonable compensation, but when he was accused, my loved one immediately shifted from wanting compensation to wanting to sue the insurance company. Although he ultimately did not do so, my own legal practice is filled with clients like him who felt compelled to pursue their claims in court after initially preferring to settle the matters amicably.

Don't let your organization end up in court unnecessarily. Listen to what the person wants and consider the problem from their perspective. Is their request reasonable? Are they alerting you to a problem that could cost you even more later if you don't address it now? Work with them cooperatively and you're liable to save your organization a great deal of money and reputation.

DUE DILIGENCE

I began this chapter by urging you to assume the best in people. I close it by reminding you to be aware of your inherent biases and how they might influence your response to reports. Do your due diligence. Trust that the people charged with investigating are doing their best, but follow up to be sure. Expect that the people who bring you problems have good intentions and need your help. Be aware of any internal biases that may be shaping how you view the allegation and the people involved.

People can be harmed in unforeseeable ways. By handling the process in a respectful, caring manner, you'll reduce the foreseeable problems and more readily resolve those that were unforeseen. Have faith in your leadership, faith in those your organization employs and serves, and faith that through compassion and curiosity, you'll find the best resolutions to even the messiest problem.

"Expect that the people who bring you problems have good intentions and need your help."

CHAPTER 8

CONSIDER AN APOLOGY

t's drilled into us from the time we get our first driver's license—never apologize, even if we caused the accident. This last idea may be the most radical and counterintuitive but, while costing you little, could have the biggest impact on your bottom line.

Apologizing, we fear, might be used against us as an admission of fault, but not doing so may become the tipping point that encourages an aggrieved party to pursue aggressive litigation and media coverage.

A friend of mine is an executive of a large and nationally renowned company. When he learned that one of his employees had been killed in a work-related accident, the lawyers for his company were firm. He was to admit nothing, have no contact with the widow, and refuse to discuss the incident. In other words, he was to be silent. Yet, he felt badly about it. He believed his company had some liability. While he understood the legal reasoning, the advice went against his personal ethics. He also knew that by remaining silent he risked a PR nightmare. So, he met with the owner of the company and they agreed to go against the legal advice of their attorneys. He visited the widow's home, offered his condolences, apologized for what had happened to her husband, and agreed that it should not have happened. He then asked what he could do to help her and her family.

The widow's request was simple: establish scholarship funds for her children who would now grow up without a father. The company did so and averted what could have become a far more costly and public settlement.

> *"Often more than anything, a person who has been wronged and who is traumatized most longs for acknowledgment of their wounds."*

Often more than anything, a person who has been wronged and who is traumatized most longs for acknowledgment of their wounds. They want those who wronged them to accept responsibility. This doesn't mean the claimant doesn't deserve compensation, but it does mean that <u>those who acknowledge the person's pain and accept responsibility are far less likely to become targets of social media attacks and high-dollar verdicts after vicious courtroom battles.</u>

In my legal practice, we only take cases with merit in which someone has been legitimately harmed or even killed due to negligence. These cases are not likely to be settled with a mere apology but, I can assure you, a client's injuries worsen when they feel the chill of an organization's refusal to acknowledge their loss with a simple, honest apology. One apology may be all it takes for a client to readily accept a settlement, whereas refusing that small gesture can push the claimant to the edge where a settlement is no longer enough.

Recall the woman in Lynnwood, Washington, who was brutally raped by a man who broke into her home and tied her up. The police not only refused to investigate the rape but also charged her with filing a false report. After surviving a brutal attack, this woman was not only convicted of the charges and fined, but was also shunned and publicly ridiculed. After the rapist attacked many more women, photographic evidence of the Lynnwood woman's rape was found in his possession. She sued the police department. Given the egregious repercussions suffered at their hand, this woman could have won a hefty settlement, but what she wanted most was to heal. She agreed to a settlement of a mere $150,000 if it came with an apology. That apology didn't cost the department a dime, but it likely saved them hundreds of thousands, if not millions of dollars.

HOW TO GIVE AN EFFECTIVE APOLOGY

Attorneys throughout the nation are rethinking the notion that a defendant shouldn't apologize. In an article for the journal, *Internal Medicine,* entitled, "Disclosing Medical Errors the Right Way," author Jessica Berthold quotes physician and Professor of Medicine Wendy Levinson: "Patients want to hear an explicit statement that an error occurred, what happened and the implications for their health, why it happened, and how recurrences will be prevented in the future for themselves and other patients. And they want an apology. Not a statement of regret like, 'I'm sorry this happened to you,' but a statement such as 'I'm sorry I caused you harm.'"[i]

---

[i] June 2014, available at: Disclosing medical errors the right way | ACP

If an apology is badly framed, it can be worse than no apology at all. The apology that essentially tells someone, "I'm sorry *you feel* I harmed you," is not heard as an apology, but as gaslighting suggesting that their feelings aren't legitimate. Similarly, the apology that's framed in passive voice and exempts the speaker from responsibility basically communicates, "Mistakes were made, but it's not my fault." This is not heard as an apology because it really isn't one. It skirts responsibility and suggests that the whole thing was just one big misunderstanding.

"An apology can be made at any point in the process, but the earlier it is made, the better."

The "if and but" apology is likewise ineffective. *"If* any harm was done, I'm sorry, *but . . .* " or *". . . but* I had no choice." These are the apologies of a cheating spouse attempting to minimize their actions, not the words of someone who is genuinely sorry and admits it never should have happened. Finally, the apology that is blurted out in frustration as in, "Look, I'm sorry this happened, but it did and there's nothing more I can do!" will

Internist "Disclosing Medical Errors the Right Way," by Jessica Berthold quoting physician Wendy Levinson, Professor of Medicine at the University of Toronto's Institute of Health Policy, Management, and Evaluation.

not make your problem go away. It will communicate that you aren't sorry but angry that you have to do something about it.

An apology can be made at any point in the process, but the earlier it is made, the better. For an apology to be effective, it must have the following elements:

- An admission that an error was made, or something happened that shouldn't have.
- An acknowledgment of how that error or action has affected the person.
- The corrective action you or your organization will take.
- A direct expression of regret or apology that is not contextualized with excuses or other linguistic signals to distance the speaker or writer from responsibility.

FIRST APOLOGIZE, THEN TAKE ACTION

After making such an apology, ask the person if they have any concerns or what more you can do to help. To the extent you can address their concerns, do so. To the extent you cannot, explain why you cannot. Finally, clearly explain what will happen next and follow up to ensure that the next steps are taken. Physician and ethicist Thomas Gallagher of the University of Washington School of Medicine emphasizes the importance of these last two steps in his quote from Berthold's article: "We've often been too focused on the words we say to patients, but in some respects, what's more important are the broader set of actions to follow."

"A financial settlement accompanied by an apology can go far in preventing litigation or, if already commenced, bringing a settlement that satisfies everyone."

These actions might be institutional change, which made a significant difference for me when program administrators at Harvard listened to some of my suggestions about revising their process. Taking action might mean correcting a material problem such as redesigning a machine or, as in the case of the 7-Eleven, putting steel bars in front of glass windows. Taking action usually means providing economic restitution and/or compensation to the victim. In my case, it was never financial compensation that I sought—it was safety. I wanted to feel safe at Harvard. I wanted to feel that they cared enough to ensure my safety by adhering to their "Community Values" and keeping predators like George out. In the cases I represent as an attorney, my clients have suffered tremendous financial losses. While emotional losses can never be undone, financial settlements are often all we can provide. A financial settlement accompanied by an apology can go far in preventing litigation or, if already commenced, bringing a settlement that satisfies everyone.

Recall the high costs of litigation reported in the first chapter of this book. Even if accepting responsibility and paying restitution is costly, it is almost always *less costly* than litigation that extends for years. Consider the countless hours your staff will spend collecting documents and testifying at depositions, and the costs to your reputation should your institution be publicly exposed as having some responsibility for the incident.

"But what happens if I apologize and they still take us to court? Won't my apology be used against me?" you might ask.

Thirty-five states already have some type of protection in the form of "apology laws" that make apologies inadmissible as evidence in court. That said, if an apology admits error, not the apology but the admission of error could be admissible, depending on state laws. This distinction remains problematic. Jeffrey S. Helmreich analyzed "apology laws" for a 2011 review article published for Cornell University Law School and noted that the laws fall short because they reinforce the idea that an apology is an admission of liability.[ii] Thus, if you are innocent and fear that an apology might be used against you, consult your state laws and err to the side of apologizing for what happened without acknowledging responsibility. Any sincere apology can still go far in demonstrating that you are not heartless, you do care, and you are willing to work with the claimant toward a resolution. Most importantly, you acknowledge their pain, which is often what they most want and need.

"Even if accepting responsibility and paying restitution is costly, it is almost always less costly than litigation that extends for years."

---

ii   Does 'Sorry' Incriminate? Evidence, Harm and the Protection of Apology (cornell.edu).

———

CASE STUDY
Ophthalmologist vs. Apology

———

In his book, On Apology, *author Aaron Lazares tells the story of an ophthalmologist who was sued after a patient attributed his loss of vision to the doctor's treatment. Although the patient felt strongly that the ophthalmologist was at fault, the doctor felt otherwise. His attorneys advised him not to apologize or express any remorse and the doctor complied. During a break in the trial, however, he ran into the patient outside the courtroom and told him, "I just want you to know that I really feel badly about how things have worked out. I don't feel that my treatment was responsible for what happened, but I do feel really bad about what has occurred, and I am concerned about you." The plaintiff returned to the courtroom and instructed his attorney to drop the lawsuit.[iii]*

———

Note what was said and not said in this apology. The doctor acknowledged that something bad happened to his patient and that he was concerned about him. He did not accept responsibility. In fact, he said clearly that he didn't feel it was fault. Notice that he didn't say he "was not" but that he didn't "feel" he was at fault—shifting the statement from an arguable point to an expression of his personal feelings. That encounter, which happened early in the doctor's career, influenced how he handled patient concerns from then on. Not only did his expression of remorse bring the lawsuit to a close, but the lesson he

---

iii Lazares, Aaron (2004), *On Apology*, Oxford University Press.

learned from it may well have prevented other potential lawsuits.

"Apologies occasionally contribute to employer liability. But almost always, those cases involved botched apologies."

Attorney Jathan Janove echoes this newer notion that apologies can lead to lower settlements or even resolve disputes altogether. "Apologies occasionally contribute to employer liability. But almost always, those cases involved botched apologies. Employer's acknowledgments of an employee's suffering, apologies for miscommunications or misunderstandings, or expressions of regret over the impact of their decisions generally have not been deemed admissions of liability."[iv] What they do is facilitate healing and resolution.

When actor James Woods' brother, Michael, died in the care of Kent Hospital in Warwick, Rhode Island, he and his nephew filed a medical malpractice case against the hospital. Woods believed so strongly in the hospital's liability that he had no intention of settling, but when the hospital president reached out to him with an apology, his hardened stance softened. The apology "made discussion possible in a case where I had no interest in settlement and was absolutely certain of victory," said

---

[iv] A 'Sorry' Strategy (shrm.org).

Woods.[v] Importantly, the apology struck Woods and his family as genuine and heartfelt, which is crucial if you want your apology to facilitate a resolution.

---

[v] Quote from article in *California Bar Journal*, Sometimes, an apology can deter a lawsuit (calbarjournal.com), by Diane Curtis.

RESOLUTION PROGRAMS SLASH LITIGATION COSTS

Stanford University Medical Center has gone so far as to institute an apology process for when things go wrong. Their "Process for the Early Assessment and Resolution of Loss" (PEARL) focuses on clearly communicating to the patient what happened, providing them with emotional counseling, and determining whether financial compensation is appropriate. The aim of the process is to minimize litigation, help identify and correct errors, and engage the patient in a healing process. Boston's Beth Israel Hospital and the University of Michigan have similar programs known as Communication and Resolution Programs (CRP). "The Michigan Model" at the University of Michigan (UM) is perhaps the leader in this field due to its own defense attorney, Rick Boothman. Boothman discovered the power of apology in reducing lawsuits and settlements and increasing patient satisfaction even when things go wrong.

In the early 2000s, Boothman was assistant general counsel and chief risk officer at UM. Weary of the "deny and defend" approach to medical mishaps and errors, he suggested a different response—acknowledge mistakes and, if deemed appropriate after performing a quality care analysis, offer immediate compensation. Three principles underlie the Michigan Model:

1. When inappropriate medical care harms a patient, they will compensate the patient or family quickly and fairly.
2. They will vigorously defend appropriate medical care.
3. By acknowledging and learning from mistakes, they will reduce patient injuries and, therefore, claims.[vi]

[vi] Boothman, Richard C. (2006), "Medical Justice: Making the System Work

"Avoiding transparency and accountability only delays and increases the costs of a settlement."

Such an approach was met with considerable resistance. After all, no one wants to admit to wrongdoing, especially physicians. People raised concerns about medical malpractice, insurance, false claims, the university, and physicians' reputations, but Boothman's hunch paid off. As Boothman noted,[vii] when a claim has merit the facts will come out in discovery. Avoiding transparency and accountability only delays and increases the costs of a settlement. By encouraging open dialogue, transparency, and accountability, the third principle of the Michigan Model proved true—patient injuries and claims significantly reduced. Medical malpractice lawsuits fell by more than half, from 2.13 per 100,000 patients to .75. New claims fell nearly as drastically, from 7.03 per 100,000 patients to 4.52. The time involved in dealing with those claims fell by a third, from eighteen down to twelve months on average. What's more, cost of claims fell by nearly half from $405,921 to $228,308.[viii]

Despite initial resistance, the Michigan Model has become a

Better for Patients and Doctors," Testimony before the U.S. Senate, Committee on Health, Education, Labor, and Pensions, June 22, 2006.

[vii] Ibid.

[viii] *Crain's Detroit Business* (2019), "Richard Boothman: Owner and Principal Boothman Consulting," May 31, 2019, available online at: Richard Boothman | Crain's Detroit Business (crainsdetroit.com).

model of cost-effective responses to patient injuries. Consequently, both doctors and litigators support the program. When testifying before the U.S. Senate in 2006, Boothman discussed a survey UM conducted of 400 physicians, noting that 98 percent supported the Michigan Model, 55 percent indicated it was a "significant factor" in their decision to stay at UM, and that plaintiff attorneys were equally impressed.

The Michigan Model is just one of many such programs across the nation. One of the first dates back to 1987 when a Veteran's Affairs (VA) hospital in Lexington, Kentucky, settled $1.5 million for two medical malpractice claims and decided it had to do something different. Then Senators Hillary Clinton and Barack Obama reported that the Kentucky VA hospital implemented a program of transparency where medical errors were disclosed to the public and patients were quickly compensated.[ix] Clinton and Obama noted that because of the program, the average cost of settling claims was $15,000 compared to $98,000 at comparable VA hospitals. Moreover, the length of time devoted to settling claims dropped from two to four years —to two to four *months*!

A 2014 study published in the journal, *Health Affairs,* noted, "These programs can substantially reduce liability costs and improve patient safety."[x] To be effective, certain features must be present including:

- Key administrators who are committed and willing to champion the program and stick with it.
- Extensive outreach to staff, training them on the values and specifics of the program.

[ix] Clinton, Hillary Rodham and Barack Obama (2006), "Making Patient Safety the Centerpiece of Medical Liability Reform," *The New England Journal of Medicine* 354(21):2205-2208.

[x] Communication-And-Resolution Programs: The Challenges And Lessons Learned from Six Early Adopters | Health Affairs.

- A culture of transparency that encourages early reporting.

"Despite initial resistance, the Michigan Model has become a model of cost-effective responses to patient injuries."

Respondents of the study noted it was difficult initially to persuade administrators and physicians to participate. Lacking an enthusiastic proponent at top levels of administration could doom a resolution program, but having one could be all that's needed to implement an effective cost-saving program.

Transparency was also a point of contention. Physicians were unaccustomed to explaining their procedures to unhappy patients and families. They also appeared to resent the time from work to attend training programs, but once they were incentivized with reductions in their insurance premiums, many grew eager to participate. Moreover, insurance carriers increasingly require early reporting of unanticipated care outcomes. Some policies even fine hospitals if carriers are not alerted to a problem until served with notice of a claim. These programs demonstrate that, contrary to conventional thinking, a sincere and properly worded apology can indeed benefit all involved.

While the trend toward CRP programs is rising in institutions and states are increasingly passing laws exempting apologies from being used as evidence in court, there is nothing new about the impact of an apology on how jurors and courts assess culpability. Nearly three decades ago, Peter H. Rehm and Denise R. Beatty published an article reviewing the legal consequences of apologies and noted, "Judges and juries seem to like apologies and treat them favorably."[xi] In cases where there were actual acknowledgments of wrongdoing, an apology was considered an admission of guilt. Where there was ambiguity, interpretation was left up to the jury. When an apology was clearly without admission of fault, as in the case with the ophthalmologist, the apology was not decisive of guilt.

"Apologizing does nothing to satisfy the plaintiff's burden of proof. In some proceedings, an apology can be a mitigating factor, and the lack of an apology can be an aggravating factor." In other words, you have little to lose by apologizing and a great deal to lose by not.

[xi] Legal Consequences of Apologizing (missouri.edu).

CONCLUSION

That evening at Harvard when I said good night to my friends and headed down the hallway to my room, I could never have imagined the radical shift that was about to occur in my thinking. In just a few minutes, my experience shifted drastically from attorney advocate to "victim." Yet, even writing the word "victim" makes me cringe. It's a word that suggests weakness and helplessness. I don't see myself or any of my clients as weak and helpless; yet, when George held me in his grip demanding that I kiss him, I felt fear. A history of past abuse returned like a torrent. It shaped the following days and weeks as I did everything in my power to create safety and ensure that Harvard acted to protect me, protect others, and acknowledge my experience and trauma.

This began not just my battle to be safe, but my cooperation with the Harvard Business School to improve how they prevent and investigate these matters. Doing so led to my writing this book so more of us know how to properly respond to reports of injury, death, harassment, or assault. And I'll be frank—my primary motivation is not to save you money. It's to help us all stop re-traumatizing people coming to us already injured. If the people who deal with claimants understand how trauma affects the brain and how the process itself can be re-traumatizing, they can see that certain methods and reactions actually cause the claimant to appear more unstable, unreliable, or untruthful. When organizations employ a trauma-informed response, the one harmed in an organizational setting will be more likely to notify personnel of potential problems or threats, and they will be better able to heal and recover.

Thankfully, this is a win-win situation because there is something in it for the institution and its employees, as well. Reforming the reporting and investigation process and establishing a trauma-informed response is constructive at multiple levels. As I've shown in these chapters, the costs to the institution or organization may be reduced, the stress and frustration of its employees can be mitigated as they deal with less stressed and defensive claimants, and the likelihood of the matter escalating to litigation may be minimized.

I want to be clear—I'm a plaintiff's attorney. When someone is harmed due to the actions, inactions, or negligence of another, and they refuse to accept responsibility, I will fight tooth and nail for them to be compensated for their suffering, and well-compensated, at that. But not everyone wants the fight. I certainly didn't. I wanted to feel safe.

For you to make the shift from an antagonistic defense to a cooperative resolution, it's important you recognize where the claimant is coming from. Allow me to share with you one final story that I think perfectly illustrates this point.

A few years back an acquaintance was attacked and bitten by her neighbor's dog. The attack terrified her and left her with permanent scarring. She filed a lawsuit. After two years of discovery and pleadings, while preparing for trial she and the attorney were discussing a demand amount. My acquaintance did not want to go to trial, but she also did not want to settle for less than six figures because in addition to the terror of being attacked and the pain and disfigurement, she'd felt further abused by having to endure a two-year legal battle.

"Can I tell you the truth?" she asked her attorney during the final settlement negotiations. "I never wanted to file a lawsuit in the first place. All I wanted was for my neighbor to put up a fence so I wouldn't have to be scared walking out to my car every day."

That simple request—to erect a fence to keep the dog in its own yard—was an expense the neighbor was unwilling to consider.

As you might imagine, the defendant ended up paying far more than the cost of a fence. Like the multi-million-dollar 7-Eleven lawsuit over the man paralyzed by the failure to install $800 worth of steel posts, the lawsuit over the fence was entirely avoidable—as were the woman's injuries.

So many of the cases that our firm takes on could have been avoided had the parties just listened to each other and considered how the other party felt, what they had experienced or suffered, and asked them what they wanted. Too often, it's this latter point that leads many to dismiss even having a serious conversation. When one party wants something from the other, a different kind of fence is erected—a psychological fence that whispers, *You won't manipulate me.*

That psychological boundary to protect us from being exploited by those with bad intent can become self-defeating if it prevents us from considering how another party is affected.

"I don't owe you anything."

"You can't make me do anything I don't want to do."

"It was an accident."

"It's not my fault."

"You're just trying to take something from me, control me, or make trouble."

These internal reactions deafen us to warning signs and

blind us to greater risks. My acquaintance's neighbor saw the request for a fence as a demand that he spend money for something he didn't want, an intrusion into what he did with his property. That defensive thinking led him to ignore the risk his neighbor was alerting him to—without a fence, the dog could hurt somebody. When the dog did attack her, the neighbor refused to take responsibility. The longer he dug in his heels, the more the damages grew.

This same thinking is even more amplified in an organizational setting where there may be hundreds if not thousands of potential parties involved. When decision makers with varied roles and interests become unwilling or unable to understand the concerns and pain of others, potential settlements can rise to millions of dollars, sometimes even bankrupting companies. The stakes are high. Because the stakes—and potential payouts—are so high, that voice that someone presenting a complaint is "just causing trouble" sometimes doesn't just whisper, it screams.

Added to that perception is how we perceive someone who has been traumatized. What might seem like no big deal to one person can be a very big deal for another. George didn't just make a pass at me I could easily dismiss. He gripped my arm so tightly it left a bruise. His actions traumatized me and, as happens with many who have been assaulted, that traumatic response didn't kick in right away. One way we survive threats is by suspending our fear. Then, once we are away from the immediate threat, the fear hits and we no longer feel safe.

So, when someone comes to you with a complaint and your first response is, "Why didn't you report it sooner?" I hope you'll think back to what you've learned in these pages. Instead of asking why they didn't report it earlier, listen to what they are reporting now.

I hope I've conveyed how the process itself can feel threatening to someone coming forward with a report of wrongdoing or harm they've suffered. By understanding how trauma affects the brain and our behavior, you will be better able to get at the truth because you will be less likely to inflict further trauma, pain, or threat on someone already traumatized.

By listening and taking the position that someone who comes to you for help is sincere, you can make the events and communications that follow so much easier on everyone, including yourself. You may also save your organization a great deal of money and reputational damage.

By changing your perception from viewing the potentially traumatized person as the problem to someone coming to you for help, you aren't failing your organization; you are serving it.

Training your staff in these trauma-informed responses that I've outlined here will not eradicate the problems your organization faces on a day-to-day basis, but doing so will make those days go more smoothly for everyone involved. And as I've stated, this will more likely safeguard your organization from avoidable lawsuits and mitigate bad publicity. You have nothing to lose from rethinking your current process and training your staff in trauma-informed responses. Indeed, you—and the organization you serve—have everything to gain from doing so. It begins with that first visit or phone call. Everything that happens afterward can lead to healing and resolution or greater trauma and escalating conflict. Which direction will your organization choose?

APPENDIX I

CHECKLIST FOR THE REPORTING PROCESS

In reviewing and analyzing your organization's reporting process, start with the frontlines. A frontline person is anyone likely to come into contact with someone reporting a problem. These frontlines include:

HOTLINES

- Is there a number for people to call if they have been injured, harassed, assaulted, or otherwise need help?
- Are there multiple numbers, organized by the nature of what is being reported?
- Are these numbers clearly posted where everyone can see them, including common areas where both men and women congregate, bathrooms, and on your websites on an easy-to-search page?
- Who answers these hotlines? Are they staffed 24/7 by employees trained in trauma-informed responses? If not, is there a recording clearly stating the hours of operation along with another number to call in case of

emergency? Or does an answering service answer these calls, where you have no control over who takes the call or how they respond?

• Are there any "black holes" in your organization regarding who you can or cannot help? Consider who could be injured or harmed while on your property or off the premises but in some way connected to you, such as a contract worker or caregiver who travels to patients' homes. These could be employees, agents, students, clients, or independent contractors to name a few. Give careful thought to any potential plaintiffs who might allege that your organization had a duty to protect or serve them, and ensure that they can easily find this hotline. Ensure that whoever answers the hotline will take their report or refer them to the appropriate person.

MANAGEMENT, SUPERVISORS, OR SPECIALTY DEPARTMENTS

This category is broad but should be obvious. Anyone in a supervisory or public-facing position should be trained to receive a complaint. It includes all managers, supervisors, HR administrators, Office of Equity and Diversity personnel, faculty, customer service, and anyone that might receive a complaint.

Depending on the type of organization, as well as the type of injury or problem, different levels of administration or management may be the first "touch" when someone is planning to make a complaint or file a report.

Be aware: people in management commonly put up the first roadblocks to resolution hoping to avoid blame for problems in their unit. Train your managers in trauma-informed responses. Teach them the detriments to your organization as I have covered in this book should they treat the complainant as the problem, and the good they will do by adhering to a respectful and trauma-informed response.

Offices of Equity and Diversity have specific categories of complaint they are charged with investigating. Ensure that they also know other units in your organization where someone can and should report a problem if it doesn't fall within their purview.

Consider inherent biases or personality traits among these managers, supervisors, and administrators to ensure that they remain objective when reports are brought to them.

Is anyone with access to a complainant likely to draw conclusions based on the social identity of the parties involved?

Do they automatically presume that certain types of reports are almost always false or manipulative, or can't possibly be true?

These types of frontline representatives can end up retaliating against someone who brings a complaint, or bury the report in such a way that if further problems come to light, their refusal to address the initial complaint puts your organization at greater legal risk.

RESOURCES

Make useful resources available early on. These resources might include:

- Counseling centers.
- Non-emergency police numbers for filing charges.
- Emergency housing.
- Crisis intervention resources.
- Hospitals and medical centers.
- Suicide prevention hotlines.
- Other resources that offer immediate help.

WRITTEN COMMUNICATION

Someone in a state of trauma may feel confused and over-whelmed by the task of putting their complaint in writing. Have intake forms or questionnaires to ensure a thorough intake of the relevant information.

- Consider appointing someone on your team to assist the complainant in completing those documents.
- Be sure the name, title, and role of any team member assisting with completion of the form or questionnaire is noted on the document.
- Make it clear that this report can be amended at any time.
- Include language explaining that completion of in-house forms is not a legal requirement, nor will it conflict in any way with anyone's legal rights.
- Are the questions clear and simple? Avoid compound questions, questions that exceed one line of text, and anything with a double-negative.
- Does the form or questionnaire ask them to revoke or limit any legal rights? This could be scary and cause someone to avoid sharing all relevant details. In this case, revise the form as needed so that it is a useful tool for *getting at* the truth, not hiding it.
- Is there a non-English-language version available? Depending on the type of organization and the people you serve, it may make sense to have translated versions available.
- Does the form ask what type of help the person needs? The more this question is asked at multiple levels of the reporting process, the better, as addressing what the *complainant* feels they need will

increase chances of resolving the matter in the early
stages.

Identify the types of help you can offer at differing points of
the reporting process. Make sure your front line people know
what to do in the event someone reports an incident that
occurred while in the care of your organization.

APPENDIX II
CHECKLIST FOR THE FACT-FINDING INVESTIGATION

Internal investigations are invariably described as "fact-finding," but let's face it. All too often they are anything but. The personalities, testimonies, and statuses of the parties involved all shape how the investigation unfolds. Should a report end up in litigation, the failure to objectively investigate the allegation can put your organization at greater risk for high damages. Moreover, a sloppy investigation can leave you exposed to further problems if someone who has harmed one person remains free to harm another. To ensure that your investigations are objective, thorough, and treat all parties humanely, offer trauma-informed training and workshops teaching anyone in an investigatory capacity how to properly conduct interviews and respond to potentially traumatized complainants.

Skilled interviewers know how to obtain information by creating a safe space and a cooperative environment. Ask open-ended questions. Listen for key words and notice vague descriptions that can be followed up with a request for more detail. If you do need to ask a follow-up question, first respond without showing judgment. Then, return with an open-ended question that encourages more conversation. For example, "He was intimidating" is vague, but following up with, "In what way?" will encourage the speaker to say more. "I was nervous" can be vague, but following up with, "I understand. Can you tell me more about that?" may lead them to share about a past trauma that is influencing how the events were experienced. Here are some more examples.

"She was really mean."

"In what way?"

"She mocked me."

"How?"

"She said I was too stupid to understand."

"Did she do or say anything else that made you feel mocked?"

"Well, she shoved me aside."

"I'm always cautious around these kinds of men."

"You said you were 'always cautious around these kinds of men.' Can you give me some examples?"

"No one would believe me."

"Why do you feel that way?"

"I come from a different background."

"Can you tell me more about that?"

"I thought I had to do it."

"Why?"

"I didn't believe him."

"Why not?"

"He grabbed me."

"Where?"

"On my arm."

"And where did this happen?"

"Outside my room."

"The car stopped at the light."

"How do you know that?"

"I saw the brake lights."

Interviewers must never appear judgmental. They must maintain eye contact, their body language open and trusting and in no way antagonistic such as glaring, leaning forward, laughing in a mocking tone, pointing fingers, or shaking their heads showing doubt in what they are hearing. Sometimes, you may need to follow up by repeating the same question in different ways. In my examples, you may notice I relied on general questions and phrases that you may want to use often, such as:

- "In what way?"
- "How do you know that?"
- "Can you tell me more about that?"
- "Why (or why not)?"
- "When did this happen?" "What time was it?
- "How?"
- "How do you recall that happening?"
- "Where?" "Where did this happen?"
- "Where were you standing?" "Where was he?" "How close were you?"
- "Can you give me some examples?"

Also crucial to a successful process is not only what you ask, but the tone in which you ask it. If something sounds unclear or off, rather than interrogate the interviewee, kindly ask for clarification. Explain your confusion in a nonjudgmental manner or make a note to return to the question at another time.

Other imperatives of an objective fact-finding investigation include:

- Treat all parties equally by sharing information with the parties equally. For example, if interviews with one party are recorded, ensure that interviews with all parties and witnesses are recorded.
- Contact <u>everyone's</u> witnesses. It's surprisingly common for investigations to exclude the witnesses of one party while contacting the witnesses another party has identified. Doing so results in skewed findings.
- Interview witnesses from inside and outside of the organization. Policies stating that only witnesses currently within the organization will be contacted precludes talking to people who may have valuable information to share such as prior employees with similar experiences, witnesses who've since left, and others who may not be associated with the organization but have information or evidence relevant to the investigation.
- Ensure that the investigative findings are recorded in an objective manner avoiding omission of reported details, inappropriate or premature conclusions, or descriptive terms that will shape the reader's perceptions of the party being interviewed.
- Review any past litigation that alleged a sloppy or biased investigation. Assign someone to review a few investigations, comparing notes and recordings to the investigators' reports.
- Establish a healthy reporting schedule for investigators with anyone overseeing the process.

Overly controlling and micromanaging the process hampers progress. Conversely, little to no involvement can cause or be indicative of a problem. Is the person overseeing the investigation happy with an occasional check-in so long as findings keep the organization innocent of responsibility, in which case you're likely to find some of these claims end up in the courts?

- As much as possible, appoint mature and experienced leadership with a trauma-informed perspective to oversee the investigative process. Investigators need someone they can turn to for clear and objective guidance, not a CYA approach that will do more to bury problems than resolve them.

Finally, even with the best staff and training, you may need to be ready with a backup plan. What will you do if the accused is personally associated with the investigators or their supervisor? Do you have alternative options, such as external investigators? If so, vet and make sure these investigators are objective. Is their continued business with your organization dependent on quashing problems rather than finding the facts? For all the reasons demonstrated in this book, an objective investigation is not only the most humane approach, but also the most beneficial to you and your organization.

APPENDIX III
DELIVERING THE FINDINGS

One of the least discussed aspects of internal investigations regards how the findings are delivered. Inevitably, someone is going to be disappointed and rarely is anyone thrilled. The incident itself was traumatic or disturbing enough to lead to a report. Then, the parties were forced to reveal and relive the incident, which may include embarrassing details.

No matter how humanely and compassionately conducted, investigations are uncomfortable and can trigger more trauma for everyone involved. To provide enough information, they may need to disclose private information including personal emails and texts. They are often required to reveal the names of friends, colleagues, and others who may have been witnesses or have useful information. Consequently, it's not at all unusual for one or more of the parties to find their friends and colleagues becoming more distant or even shunning them.

For these reasons, how and when you deliver the findings makes a difference. I know in my case I was shocked to learn that George would not be removed from the program, mostly because I'd been led to believe otherwise. Later, when I learned he'd reapplied to the program, I relived that same shock because I was treated as if I was some random person with no standing in the matter. Refusing to tell me information directly relevant to my claim and my interests caused my anxiety and anger to escalate. Fortunately, someone did listen to me. When I learned that George would not be readmitted, I relaxed. My point here is that investigations can take weeks or months, and in some cases even years, during which the parties live with heightened anxiety, loss of sleep, and often fear. Delivering findings they won't like can turn that anxiety into an emotional explosion, which no one wants. To mitigate such a possibility, ensure that your findings:

- Are delivered to all parties at the same time so no one learns about it through social media or the grapevine.
- Do not disparage or discredit the claimant, even if the findings do not support his or her claim. Characterizing the claim as unfounded, untrue, malicious, absurd, or ridiculous, or the claimant as lying, dishonest, or otherwise attacking their character will escalate the battle. They will feel re-traumatized and will take further steps to restore their dignity and reputation.
- Characterize the evidence, not the people involved. "The evidence we were able to collect and review was insufficient to support the claim," may not go over well with the one who made the claim, but it is far better than saying, "The claim was unfounded," or "The claimant could not prove that anything happened." Keep the findings focused on the evidence, not the people.
- Include directives for any appeals.
- Include suggested remedies, consequences, or punitive measures wherever applicable.

- Are consistent with local and federal laws.
- Are discreet and respect the confidentiality of everyone involved.

Finally, do not put undue expectations on the parties to obtain or learn the findings. Be sure they are delivered in a timely manner and, as I've said above, to all parties at the same time. Telling someone they must come to you to obtain the findings might make sense if they are nearby and you want to deliver difficult news in person, but if they must travel a long distance or have childcare, work, or other commitments or obstacles making that difficult, then deliver the news electronically or by mail. Don't make them wait. Telling someone you've made your decision at the end of the day on Friday and will deliver it on Monday causes unnecessary anxiety. Tell them on Monday.

In the same vein, don't keep telling them you're almost done if you aren't. Give a realistic timeline. If for any reason there's a delay, let them know. When you do have a finding, deliver it in writing even if also telling them in person. Focus on the evidence and procedures, not the character of the people, and use compassionate language void of judgment. While the findings are a form of judgment, your language need not be.

Being aware that the process can be slow, emotionally taxing, and greatly impact the lives of everyone involved, you have the power to minimize the negative toll it takes on their lives and emotions. Practice this greater awareness and implement a trauma-informed response to mitigate damages and create a win-win situation for everyone.

ACKNOWLEDGMENTS

To the guys that fill my heart and give life meaning . . .

Mike, you are the kindest and most patient person I have ever known. I am blessed to have had the privilege of calling you my husband for the past twenty-five years. You're the one who knows me best and still chooses me unconditionally. I would not be who I am today had you not been by my side. Thank you for loving me through all the moments of life, especially the tough ones.

I was trying to remember the moment I first told you my thoughts about writing a book but couldn't recall. You probably do. I think it's because we've had so many conversations that start with me saying, "Hey, I wanted to talk to you about something I'm thinking about doing . . . " Sometimes you give me the side eye; sometimes you just laugh and ask what we're doing next. One day you told me, "It's just the way you are, Becky. Whenever life gets calm for a minute, you get uncomfortable and need to do something to shake it up." Truer words have never been spoken.

As a man that fully enjoys calm and peace, this way of living has not always been easy for you. When a calm moment of life stirred my desire to go to Harvard Business School, we talked about me going to Cambridge for the last six weeks of the program. Without hesitation, and despite that it put more pressure on you with your own work and our responsibilities at home, you fully supported me. This was an enormous sacrifice that you never once named. I need to name it now and tell you that I will forever be indebted to you for this gesture of love. There is no measure great enough to describe my gratitude to you. I can make you one promise: I will try to do less things in the next twenty-five years that make your butt pucker. *I will try.*

I will love and treasure you always.

Jake and Justin, you are the eternal lights of my life. I thank God every day for making me your mom. There is no greater joy and no more important thing that I will ever do in my lifetime. As different as you are, you share so many characteristics. Both of you are incredibly funny, kind, smart, competitive, sarcastic, and loving. It is so much fun and such a wild ride watching you grow up. Your age gap has allowed me and Dad one-on-one time with each of you and, now that Jake has graduated from college, we get to experience the true joy of having the whole family back together. Time is fleeting, and I have appreciated and loved every single second. These are days I will always cherish and will not take for granted.

I cannot wait to see the paths you choose for your lives. I know they will be your own choices and not those that others may want for you. It would be impossible for either of you to escape the genetic trait of strong-mindedness passed down from both me and your dad. You have made your own decisions, according to your own timetables, and in your own ways. My hope is that each of you always follows your heart, chases your dreams, has fun, works hard, and knows true love.

Reggie, a.k.a. Reginald Muffin, you are my puppy-face baby dog, our sweet stray that was found behind a dumpster in Tennessee and delivered to us via the Humane Society Love Train. You are the sleepiest dog of all time, paired with the best zoomies. You're either on one hundred, or all tuckered out. My true spirit animal. I woof you.

To the amazing woman that helped me create this book . . .

When I came up with the idea, I sat down and wrote an

outline because that's what a book writing website told me to do to begin my journey as an author. I was clever and named the chapters as if they were case headings (Risk v. Reward, Opportunity v. Threat, etc.). I'm a lawyer, you know, so I knew it was the most creative and awesome thing ever.

After drafting the outline and elaborating on the chapter ideas, I quickly realized I had no idea how to write a book, so I began the search for a writing coach. It was important I found someone who really understood my intent and how critical it was to get the messaging right. After speaking with several people, I was introduced to the most wonderful, intelligent, uniquely perfect person.

Janice Harper, I thank you from the bottom of my heart. You took one look at that amazing outline I wrote and told me what a piece of crap it was (in a much nicer manner), and then proceeded to guide me through the maze of book writing. There were so many deeply personal topics that we needed to discuss. You were kind and professional and made it easy. In the two years we worked together, you always provided honest feedback and great insight. You brought a complementary perspective to my ideas and offered many of your own. Your life's work provided depth and context to the book, and to my life in general. I truly appreciate you and cannot wait to get started on our next project together.

HiGHERLIFE
PUBLISHING & MARKETING

PUBLISHING · MARKETING · BRAND DEVELOPMENT

IF YOU'RE A FAN OF *WIN WIN*, WILL YOU HELP SPREAD THE WORD?

There are several ways you can let others know about *WIN WIN*…

- Post a 5-Star review on Amazon.
- Write about *WIN WIN* on your social media accounts.
- If you podcast or blog, consider referencing *WIN WIN*, or publish an excerpt with a link back to the website: www.rebeccasposita.com.
- Recommend *WIN WIN* to friends. Word of mouth is still the most effective form of advertising.
- Purchase additional copies to distribute or sell to clients, prospects, team members, donors, brokers, dealers, associates, co-workers, family, and friends.

www.ingramcontent.com/pod-product-compliance
Lightning Source LLC
Chambersburg PA
CBHW071556210326
41597CB00019B/3278